The
168 Hour Week

Living Life
Your Way
24-7

Praise for The 168 Hour Week

"This is the REAL book about work, productivity, happiness, and profit. In four hours you will discover answers for a lifetime of success and fulfillment." *--Jeffrey Gitomer, author of The Little Red Book of Selling*

"The most scientific book ever written on personal productivity." *-- Mark Joyner, #1 Bestselling Author of Simpleology and Founder of Construct Zero*

"What you've been told causes success is flat-out wrong! Kevin Hogan explains why you haven't gotten the results you've wanted. More importantly he shows you how to leverage the latest scientific *breakthroughs to really succeed in life*. Get this book as if your success depended on it – because it does!" *--Rich Schefren, CEO, Strategic Profits*

"Forget goal setting and time management as you know it. If you need to make meaningful, profitable change in your life or career right now, read this book. Actionable, profitable information based on the latest psychological science interpreted as only Dr. Hogan can. Read this book now and change your life for the better . . . forever!" *-- Dave Lakhani Author of How To Sell When Nobody's Buying and Power of an Hour: Business And Life Mastery In One Hour A Week*

"I don't know anyone who can communicate with greater skill, power, and compassion than Kevin Hogan. In fact, after reading his latest book, I'm convinced he's the "Bruce Lee" of the personal development. *The 168 Hour Week* reads like a cross between *Enter the Dragon* and *Think and Grow Rich*. Grounded in reality, backed by research, and packed with powerful strategies and tactics, you can't help but read it and come away ready, willing, and able to kick some serious ass. And even in today's uncertain times, with the right knowledge and the right spirit, it is still possible to live our lives on our own terms. Don't believe me? Read *The 168 Hour Week* and you will." *--Blair Warren, Television Producer www.blairwarren.com*

"I am sorry, but you mustn't read Kevin's latest book - if you still plan to excuse yourself for procrastinating or achieving less than you could...Deep lasting change after reading another book???

No! This is not "another book". It's unlike anything you've ever read on the subject. Concoction of scientific data, unique metaphors and humor makes it irresistible. You won't need any excuses any more..." *--Ewa Zaremba, CEO Masters Educational Co., Poland, life-masters.com.pl*

 "Kevin takes a big crate of dynamite and blasts conventional time management topics-- goal setting, planners, scheduling, procrastination, outsourcing, etc--- down to solid bedrock to uncover and reveal what REALLY matters... *If this book can't turbo-charge your life, focus your dreams, and accelerate your achievement nothing can...* This is a Bible of Achievement for the 21st Century..." *--Rob Northrup, President, Advanced Extrusion Solutions*

"Most books on time management and goal setting say the same things. The problem is that most of what they say simply doesn't work in the 'real world'. This book is different. Kevin Hogan has taken an enormous amount of scientific research and distilled it down into an easy-to-use system anyone can use to take control of their lives and achieve their dreams. In the hands of someone who will apply the information contained within it, this is a powerful and life-changing book." *--Steve Chambers, President, SMOS Companies, Inc.*

"Kevin Hogan, internationally known for sharing scientific research in bite-sized chunks that can be immediately implemented, has *written the master productivity primer* for creating the life you want. If you are sick and tired of bleeding away your time, your energy and your dreams while the days and years fly by, STOP…and read this book. Hogan pulls no punches in helping you truly 'get' that you are in charge of your time and your life and he walks you through a step-by-step process to greater freedom and empowerment. Honor yourself today by using this book to take action toward a better life – YOU are worth it!" *--Mollie Marti, Ph.D., Founder - BestLifeDesign.com. Author, The 12 Factors of Business Success*

"Is this Kevin Hogan's best book yet? This book is written from passion with passion, based on scientific research, written in simple language with humor thrown in. He has created a step by step system that will help you transform your life through understanding Procrastination, Time Management and Goal Achievement. If you want to know if you have encountered Mr Zen, or Mr Critic or even Mr Chaos so far in your life and if you want to know how *to get out of the*

'Hamster Wheel', you need to read this book cover to cover and follow through. But be warned. This book can change your life. This book has been an absolute joy to read. Thank you, Kevin Hogan for writing it and sharing your knowledge." *--Lena Georgiades – Fashion Designer and Technician. United Kingdom*

"Proven principles and practical advice written by an author who reveals the formula to break free from what holds you back from ultimate success. Hogan provides the blueprint to create the life plan you desire, identify and eliminate what prohibits success and most importantly how to live the life you deserve. A must read for everyone." *--Eliot Hoppe – CEO of Paramount Learning, Alberta, Canada; and Author of Selling: Powerful New Strategies for Sales Success*

"Kevin Hogan doesn't see you through his eyes, but yours. He helps you make a difference and realize the greatest dreams. With the book, time comes to your side." *--WEN Zhen, European Commission Delegation. Candidate for United Nations Competitive Examinations for Translators and Interpreters, Beijing China*

"Once I got this book, I literally couldn't put it down. I spent my day reading it until it was finished - and I'm so glad I did. As a person who wants to get as much out of my day as possible, and always wondering why I wasted any time doing things that I shouldn't be, this book was a God send. *Kevin pulls back the curtains on why we procrastinate so much in our daily activities* and reveals why we're not as productive as we know we can be. His simple approach breaks everything down into easy to understand pieces so that you can see where you can implement what is needed for you to be productive, and more importantly, successful. What you learn will put you on the road to productive success, but will change how you schedule your day so that not only are your working hours more productive, but so are your non working ones, too. A must read for anyone wanting to overcome Procrastination and have their productivity go through the roof - so much so that I'm off to read it again!" *--David Walsh, United Kingdom CEO - ProductLaunchConsultancy.com*

"Another Masterpiece by Kevin Hogan! Finally a book that delivers proof debunking time 'management' myths and delivers practical solutions that work for busy people in the real world of business. Kevin reveals a simple system to blast procrastination habits forever. Read

this book today and gain the competitive edge over 93% of corporate executives while you get control over your life back!"
--Deborah Micek, CEO, RPMsuccess.com, New Media Strategist and Author of Secrets of Online Persuasion

"Just about everything you have been told about time management, motivation and goal setting is flat out wrong. Get ready for some in your face changes and planning that will help increase action in your business and personal life. Kevin has laid out in an easy to read and easy to use workbook on how to achieve the life you know that you are capable of. It is up to you whether you will live up to being the person you know you can be. Write in your book, mark it up and then implement what you learn immediately". *--Scott S. Bell, Senior Technician and Sales Trainer, Bell Brothers HVAC, www.definedimpact.com*

"You can start throwing out your old goal setting books because Kevin Hogan has written the no B.S. Guide to goal setting and destroying procrastination. I defy you to read Chapters 6 + 7 and not feel like you just got the kick in the ass you need to take action now! This is the success blueprint for the rest of your life." *--Michael D. Walker, CEO, ZentiMental.com and Production Team Member Cirque du Soleil's Zumanity*

"An invigorating read, clearly written with personal passion; full of invaluable life success tactics. I do live my life 'my way' and I've loved every moment of it since I discovered how to (just to do it!). Still, I struggle with procrastination, time management, frustration and sometimes lose sight of my vision or goals. Kevin's simply implemented strategies, and well structured time management plans, were exactly what I needed to move on to the next level with my own personal development, maximizing my productivity, i.e. success. A much needed tier addition to my life toolbox. This is a terrific read for anyone, but especially those wishing to better organize their time, gain motivation and clarity for the journey to reach their goals, and live a fuller, happier life knowing and appreciating who they are. There are many books about personal development but this is the only I have came across which is written in such a pure, non frills approach. Everyone needs to know about this life changing book." *--Laurena Lacey, International Model, www.laurenalacey.com*

A Simple System to Blast Past Procrastination, Meet Your
Goals and Make Your Dreams Come True

The
168 Hour
Week

Living Life
Your Way
24/7

Kevin Hogan

Be Who You Want to Be, Live Where You Want to Live, Have
Everything You Deserve in Life

The 168 Hour Week: Living Life Your Way 24/7
Hogan, Kevin, 1961-
The 168 Hour Week: Living Life Your Way 24/7

Foreign Rights inquiries welcome. E-mail: meta@ix.netcom.com

Library of Congress Cataloging-in-Publication Data
Hogan, Kevin.
The 168 Hour Week: Living Life Your Way 24/7
Kevin Hogan.
Includes bibliographical references.

1. Quality of work life. 2. Part-time self-employment. 3. Self-
Realization 4. Self-Actualization 5. Quality of Life.
I. Title. II:Title: 168 Hour Week. III. Title: Living Life Your Way
24/7
HD6955.H63   2009
650.1 --dc22   2006

ISBN 13: 978-1-934266-14-4
ISBN 10: 1-934266-14-0

Printed in the United States of America

Cover Design by Elle Phillips

First Edition

Printing number

10 9 8 7 6 5 4 3 2 1

For Katie, Mark and Jessica

Contents

Acknowledgments

Many thanks to: Bryan Lenihan, Eliot Hoppe, Rob Northrup, Steve Chambers, Sonya Lenzo, April Braswell, Darryl Pace, Craig Ernst, David Power, Rhonda Brooks, Esther Ames, Sabrina Peterson, Yann Vernier, John Ho, Bob Kaufer, John Bedosky, and Scott Bell.

Deep appreciation to: Ken Owens, Lisa McLellan, Gail Hurt, Jennifer Battaglino, Michelle Matteson, Mark Ryan, Dave Lakhani, Rebecca Joy, Elsom Eldridge, Phil Hamilton, Phil Graves, Terence and Julie Watts, Andrzej Batko, Devin and Rachel Hastings, Scott and Carmen Schluter, Paul and Rosie Schluter, JP and Deb Micek, Todd Bramson, Mollie Marti, Gary May, Larry Adams, Bob Beverley, Blair Warren, Mishelle Shepard, Kate McKeon, Michael Walker, Mark Hendricks, George Flinn, Karl Morris, Al Duncan, Eric Knowles, Stewart Emery, Bill Harris, David Garfinkel, Mike Morgan, Mark Victor Hansen, Lena Georgiades, David Walsh, Elle Phillips, Ewa Zaremba, and Laurena Lacey.

A deep bow to: Jeffrey Gitomer, Mark Joyner, Rich Schefren and Jay Abraham.

Most importantly for fine tuning, working and reworking the manuscript several times and doing everything... Katie Hogan.

For the dozens of amazing people I neglected to identify here, get on my back and make sure I get you in the next book out in Spring! I appreciate you! For the readers of *Coffee with Kevin Hogan* - you are the best.

Any mistakes in the book are mine.

Foreword by Mark Joyner

I t's not often that books about personal productivity are written by people who have genuine scientific knowledge about the way the human mind works.

Even less often that they are written in a way that you can easily understand and immediately implement.

The book you hold in your hands fits that bill and I can count on one hand the books in the world that do. Among them, however, this book is the most scientific. Being a close personal friend of Kevin's, it's easy to forget that he is one of the most accomplished men alive in the field of human psychology. He's far too humble to wear that on his sleeve.

You'll forget that, too, as you read this book. It's so easy and accessible you'll forget it was written by one of the greatest minds alive. And I mean that in the best way possible.

Great writing does not call attention to itself or impress you with the author's knowledge - instead it does something far more important: it brings out the greatness in you that has been waiting there all along.

This is one of those books and I won't waste another moment of your time with this foreword. That time will be far better spent getting started. So, let's do that now...

Mark Joyner

Introduction

Can You Really Live Your Life, Your Way?

C an you have everything you want in life?
That word "everything" is a really big word.
Within specific boundaries and certain parameters, you can have almost everything you want in life. I'd like to show you *how to be where YOU want to be in YOUR life.*
What will you learn in this book?
You will learn that if you can "be real" about the life you dream of and desire, you can have it.

...It was just one of those conversations two friends have until one of the most brilliant people on the planet, my friend Richard Brodie, who "invented" Microsoft Word and later authored *Virus of the Mind...*said, "You know, you ARE the most productive person I've ever met." And he worked with the most productive company at its genesis...it's most productive time. Richard never just says anything. He thinks about everything he says. He's intellectually meticulous in a way that I am jealous of to this day. I don't know that he was right about me, but of the two or three questions people ask me, one of them is "how do you get so much done?"

To live life your way, you'll find out how to break free of what holds you back. And you do that by following the simple steps to:

a) **Reduce Procrastination**
b) **Increase Productivity using a Time Planning System that actually works.**
c) **Integrate Key PEOPLE into your Life**
d) **Know Who You Are...and Find Out Where You Want to Be**

This book is a "formula" for having What You Want 168/24/7.
It is a formula for Living Life Your Way
It is a formula to have all; to be all that you want to be.

It is a formula for having a life with meaning.

Ultimately, this simple methodology is designed from studying mountains of not so simple research on goal achievement, enhancing productivity and overcoming procrastination.

I've done the digging for you, because if we don't take advantage of the science of achievement, we become limited to each guru's ideas of what works and what doesn't.

This book is different from any other book you've read.

You've already figured out that there are several problems with popular goal setting books, time planners and similar pop psychology stuff. Most are very well intended, many have honorable and admirable ideals, but they simply don't work in the real world.

The problem with almost all of the other work in the "reach your dreams" genre, is that the books are authored by people who don't understand how people think and what they really *want* to do in life. They truly believe that if you do what other people with great lives do, that they will get the same results. It simply doesn't work that way.

I've developed this "system" for people who want to live life on their own terms and not succumb to being "stuck." I've put this together for people who realize that using someone else's strategy is far from assurance of anything.

Example: The top golfers will all tell those asking for the secrets of their victory that they, for example, visualized success as a big part of their game. As you interview the winning golfer and he'll tell you other things he did to win. Then what happens is you go and do that same stuff and you don't win.

Why?

Every other golfer on the tour did the same rituals, the same visualizations. The people who "fail" are doing the same things as the people who are the "winners."

"Modeling" is a really important concept. You'd think that if you found out what someone else was doing and then went and did it, you'd get the same results.

It sounds so obvious.

And it doesn't work that way in real life, because modeling is all about what someone else did, what *they* believe, what *they* think, *their* sequencing of actions. And the fact is, that given a different context or a different environment or a different personal history or a different wife or a different automobile, or a different boss or a different domed stadium....well...the model falls apart.

This doesn't mean we stop asking achievers what they do and how they do it, you just don't fall into the trap that one author did in his book, about companics that were at the pinnacle of their success in the 80's and 90's. The author did painstaking data collection and tons of interviews from pretty much all the top companies from the 20 years he analyzed. The book became a cornerstone of a million libraries.

Sadly, the information that was collected wasn't the necessary information for determining greatness or success in companies. In the ensuing decade after the release of the book, the companies that had been truly spectacular were no more than average in growth or stock value.

To the author's credit, he's written a follow up book having the benefit of hindsight.

But the lessons learned directly and by extrapolation from the observations made in the book and then finding out that they aren't the factors that cause greatness are shocking. These lessons are profound.

You read the book and it all "makes sense." I'm looking at it right now, and it's hard to believe that the conclusions of what makes people and companies great...is simply incomplete at best, or wrong at worst. But it all made "sense" when I read the book as it did to another million owners of businesses small and large.

The real lessons in retrospect are quite different from what the book posited originally. In real life we now know that...

1) What got you to #1, **doesn't** keep you there.
2) You must **evolve**.
3) You must never get too comfortable because **change** is coming.
4) What you **believed** got you to #1 probably didn't get you there at all.

5) There is a lot of **randomness** in life that just happens to you and me.

6) You can pick yourself up from any point and **achieve greatness** in your life.

7) More important than success is to **understand** *failure*.

8) Long-term failure is **common** to human nature.

9) If you utilize designed "**MOVING AWAY FROM**" FAILURE STRATEGIES, you will succeed.

10) The Status Quo is your desired state of mind but the world around you **requires** that you change.

It's interesting that social scientists; academicians, had this all figured out years ago.

Researchers have determined that people are lousy at analyzing themselves. People don't know why they just did whatever they did, nor what they will do next. **People have little idea where they will be as far as life is concerned in five years.**

For example: Nothing is more important than environment and context to achievement. Take the child out of one classroom and put her in another very different room and she will perform differently.

Want a specific? Take female students out of the room with male students and girls/women will perform significantly better at mathematics.

Another? Bring "black people" into a strategy meeting filled with all "white people" and people in the group as a whole make BETTER decisions.

KEYPOINT: Things commonly believed to cause achievement are almost always unimportant.

There are thousands of studies that I've pored through to shape a worldview of human behavior that is based on observation and not the personal biases of a Pastor, a Manager, a Salesperson, a Mother, or Kevin Hogan.

When you find out that success isn't caused by XYZ, you need to make sure you tell the rest of the world, because a lot of people are going to say, "Oh, that's what made Ford so great! Cool, we'll do that, too!" But it's not what made Ford great. It SEEMED LIKE IT, but there were no scientific studies and actual statistical analyses completed. And when you go looking for something, you tend to find it.

Example: People reasonably believe that leadership is really important in a company. Yes, it can be. But if you look at things objectively, you see that some of the most corrupt people helped build some of the most successful companies (success defined as market capitalization being big or stocks that went up and up and up in this case).

Character matters to me, but in most companies, it doesn't matter much to profits.

Leadership matters to me, but who is President of most, but not all, companies doesn't make a lot of difference in the success of the company in the long run.

Honesty matters to me but…you get the idea.

What if the people who "model" successful companies and successful people got the REAL ANSWERS to the questions, "Then what did you do?" and "How did you deal with that?" and "What specifically did you do next?"

An answer would be the equivalent of a record-breaking superstar in baseball coming out and saying, "I took steroids."

The real answers, the true, honest, accurate, real answers arc often what we don't want to hear.

Executives don't tell you they failed to fund the pensions, or that they based their pension projections on market returns that have *never* been matched in the past. The government doesn't tell you they built their Social Security scheme precisely as Bernie Madoff built his billion-dollar Ponzi scheme.

Part of what is unusual about this book is that it's based on the assumption that **people who achieve greatness are as defective as anyone else**, and that what the rich and famous told you made them successful…was wrong. They glossed over reality and painted it how you wanted to hear it. Or, maybe they thought that they got the life they did because they were "blessed", or for some other reason that wasn't quite on the mark.

You won't get that in this book.

This book is radical because I have an agenda. **I have decided to be the first person to tell you the truth about time planning, time management, goal setting, procrastination and achievement.**

Don't think that means that everything will be different from what you have read in the past. That isn't going to happen. You'll simply see what works, what really matters.

Even though character, honesty, and thoughtful leadership don't really correlate to market cap or stock price success, I would prefer that you adopt characteristics of goodness rather than otherwise.

It makes the world a better place and as crazy as that sounds, it means a lot to me as a person.

That said, you won't read any BS in this book. When I tell you I am motivated by something like sex, for example, you don't need to gasp and pretend that I have said anything all that surprising. I promise you that the more accurately you portray your Self to your Self, the more likely you are to get what you want in life. And you can always be frank with me. Always.

Nevertheless you will be surprised and startled at times as you turn the pages of this book. You'll find out that *sometimes* common sense isn't common. You'll also find out that some stuff from conventional wisdom ***does work*** in real life. You'll discover that some doesn't.

I will never give you a bogus pep talk. Professional Coaches don't BS their players. They know their players. They draw plans. They make contingencies. They have backup players that are ready to go. The team with the better players will win more than they lose, but if two teams players are exactly the same in execution, the team with the better plan, plays and contingencies will win. That would be you.

Finally, every now and then I will mention a program or a live event that I have developed that I think might be useful for you to know about. There are no 1-800 numbers in this book. But the programs that are noted are noted because there is breadth and depth in those specific areas that go far beyond what you can do in a 300-page book. Some things you simply can't "read into being."

You picked up this book because you want to do one of the few things that every human being really does deserve. You want to live they life you want.

Today, you begin.

Chapter One

Choosing a REAL Lifestyle

I t seems pretty simple, right?
        You would think...

If you decide what you really want in life, you'll choose to do that instead of some of the things you are doing now.

In fact, as you think about the things you want in life, you should be more excited and optimistic about your life.

And you would think that getting these things you really want might be a little work but not all that difficult, and even if it was difficult you'd still "go for it" because you really do want this other kind of life.

So setting up the time to make all that stuff happen just makes sense and if you do a little each day toward getting that life or those things, then eventually you'd "get there."

You would set goals for stuff you want, or a life you want to live.

You would stop procrastinating because these are things that "motivate you."

You would be more productive because you'd enjoy doing the things it takes to get to the Promised Land.

You would find it easy to manage your time, stay on task, being able to push aside the daily interruptions of life because these are choices you are making, completely of your own imagination, thought, desires, and interests. No one is telling you where to go or what to do, or how to do it.

It makes sense.

So you go buy a planner and start to organize your life and fill in all the time slots so you know what you'll be doing each day.

You set aside time for working toward the life you are creating, or even toward creating your own work instead of being a hamster in someone else's wheel.

It should work.

Unfortunately, it doesn't.

You did all the things that "made sense" and they didn't work.

KEYPOINT: The biggest reason we don't feel the need to change our life, to select a better way to live, is because we don't understand the concept of time and, more specifically, our lifetime.

What Goes Wrong With Traditional Time Management Strategy?

You became even more overwhelmed with life and because you can't just up and quit your job, *you carved out all the stuff from your planner that you had dreamed of, wanted, desired, and decided to stick with how things are now*. Sure life is overwhelming but you haven't made it more overwhelming by taking on even more stuff.

You then determined that being extremely overwhelmed was making you unhappy. And you decided that you were happy enough right now. **People perceive that the most important time is now.**

And sometimes that is certainly true. And you could easily argue that "now" is a lot more important than the past. After all, the past IS gone. It's history. It's done. It might be rewritten but it won't be played out again, except in your mind. You could argue that focusing on the past is a waste....of time.

And you could argue, because life is short, and it is, that everything that happens tomorrow is tomorrow. "Tomorrow will take care of itself." I've heard that, you've heard that.

What matters is today, this moment, right now. Live NOW because you might not be here tomorrow.

You know what?

All of the above is often true and often accurate.

So people decide that they will have fun today, relax today, be less stressed today, go boating today, go party today, go hang out today...and well...you get the idea.

After all we have determined that it makes sense.

And you don't need to go buy a daily planner whether it works or not if you are living in the moment. Life will come to you and you will meet it when it gets to you.

Relief breaks out. Just reading what I wrote above, actually makes me relax and feel calm. My body sort of leaves a state of stress and move to peace. What could POSSIBLY be wrong with that?

KEYPOINT: To live the life you want, you want to see life as it really is.

The Well Concealed Facts of Real Life

If you live alone, have no problem with transitional housing, are willing to live in high risk neighborhoods, not have a spouse, not have a job, not have stuff...if your health is perfect and will stay perfect, if you are willing to abandon your kids or having kids, if you are OK with gambling on the government to keep you safe, secure and taken care of....then you can give the Traditional Time Management Hope Strategy a shot before starting a family or living with someone. I'd prefer you to live the life the way YOU want to live it.

Most people prefer to have someone to share life with, to live in a safe neighborhood, eat decent food, and have a fairly normal, if not good, life.

Having "enough" is a disturbing trend I've seen in the pop psychology literature lately. It disturbs me because most people believe that "enough" is when your current income is greater than your current expense.

That is not "enough." That is one step from falling off a cliff. It is a grand illusion to consider otherwise.

Let's say you currently earn $7,000 per month and your expenses are $7,000 per month. Imagine that being an astute individual you think long term and stash 10% of that money into a retirement account that will grow tax deferred until you withdraw the money.

Living paycheck to paycheck is probably one of the biggest red flags you can see in your life. This gives birth to more crises than just about any other controllable factor in life.

Paycheck-to-Paycheck Problem One

Let's say you are married or will be married and have or will have 2 kids. (The probability is very high you will become married if you aren't and the probability is very high that you will have children when you do get married.)

You are living within your means. Your job is providing a decent living. Sure you don't like your job but you HAVE a job and live better than most people in the country do.

So what is wrong with the picture?

For today, the picture is pretty good.

Now let me just throw out some scenarios that have happened in my life and let's see what happens. Imagine you or your spouse dies. How does that affect things?

Kind of makes life change on a dime. Now you (assuming your spouse died and not you) need to replace your spouse's income. You have two kids who will prefer a parent to a 14-hour per day babysitter but their preference won't matter because you'll be working 8-5, then somewhere else 6-11. You won't see your kids.

How likely is such a scenario?

It happens often enough for my Mom to have survived my Step Dad passing away, when I was the oldest of five at age 12, and when my Mom was 8 years old, her Mom died, leaving her Dad with …two children and no Mother. That's just my Mom's side of the family…. Things were much more difficult on my Father's side of the family.

Someone dies and your household income is cut in half. Your paycheck-to-paycheck life is now over. Does this happen 10% of the time? Probably not. It is obvious that not being prepared for when someone who supports the family dies is like throwing people into a Hurricane.

Paycheck-to-Paycheck Problem Two

Next thing that could happen is the Abandonment Divorce. There are a lot of "types" of divorce. Divorce shreds a family at the core of love, stability, time, money; you name it. Living paycheck to paycheck and then getting a divorce is the same as having a breadwinner die. The only difference is there is a lot more hostility and anger to live with. However, worse than having hostility and anger with no paycheck is when the other parent completely abandons the kids...as in gone. As in no financial support, no love, no nothing.

Divorce happens to about 40% of marriages. Maybe more. Very few survivors of those marriages can even pay their bills after a divorce without remarrying or taking money from the government.

The Abandonment Divorce is not as popular as the Live Next Door Divorce but I hazard to guess that about ¼ of all divorces result in one person leaving everyone behind.

The person who leaves, of course, can then pursue the 4 Hour Work Week because they have no responsibilities, no bills. They are living in the moment and free...Zen...letting life come to them...at peace.

Meanwhile the person left with the 2 (or more) kids is in a real situation. Just think right now, how would you get by? Really?

Yes, divorce happened to my Mom, twice, one was an Abandonment Divorce that left her with 3 kids and zero dollars. Divorce happened to me personally but I wasn't living paycheck to paycheck. That said, divorce shakes your world in ways you can't imagine. Everything you dream about that is good can vanish in an instant leaving a completely different future than you can imagine.

40+%

Those are really good odds...and a really good reason to NEVER live paycheck to paycheck.

The Paycheck-to-Paycheck Problem Three

Disability. You are about SEVEN times as likely to become disabled for more than 3 months this year, than you are to die. Most people assume they have disability insurance until they find out they didn't know what disability insurance was. They think it kicks in automatically when you become disabled. That's not the case. Usually 3-6 months after someone becomes disabled, it begins. Then how much do you get from insurance? About half of what your income was. So 3-6 months with no income and then half of the income.
Most divorced people with kids can't survive this scenario without a shattered world. If there were two incomes prior to the disability, you can often credit card your way to bankruptcy and survive.

And yes, this one happened to my first AND second step dad. My first step dad was disabled for three YEARS (no insurance) and my second step dad was disabled for two YEARS. There was a policy that kicked in after three months in that case.

What are the odds?

If you are 25 there is a 44% chance you will have at least one long-term disability prior to age 65.

Once you hit age 40 there is a 39% chance you will have least one long-term disability prior to age 65.

And at age 50, there's a 33% chance you will have at least one long-term disability prior to age 65.

And obviously you are wondering how long before most people recover from their disability and can get back to work, say five years after becoming disabled.

Age of Onset	Recovered	Died	Still Disabled
24	44%	10%	46%
35	34	12	54
45	21	20	59
55	12	28	60

In a nutshell, the chance of disability at age 40 is about 40% and 70% of those people are dead or still disabled at age 45.

Women who become disabled are THREE TIMES more likely to than men to become out of work due to disability.

Disability often has a "cap" or an "end date" on it, by the way.

And to the credit of people, most disabled people go back to work at some point in their life and earn about ½ of what able-bodied people earn.

About half the people who file for bankruptcy are disabled.

About 8,000,000 American's are disabled in accidents each year.

Most people who don't read scientific literature will tell you that it's smart to wait to have a family. That is the current trend. It's an instant gratification time management problem. It's also a really bad idea.

Paycheck to Paycheck Problem Number Four

Unemployment is the final big life crusher. The fact is that millions of American's become unemployed (fired) each year. When you don't have a job, you don't have money, which means you probably end up in foreclosure or close. "Losing a job" is not quite as common as becoming disabled, but they run neck and neck.

The Paycheck-to-Paycheck Life Solution

If you are living Paycheck to Paycheck, trying to add "balance" to your life, you have been watching Oprah too much.

As you can see between, death, disability, divorce and being fired, you can't live paycheck to paycheck and have a stable life or state of mind.

The only smart way to live life is to create a life where you no longer have to live paycheck to paycheck.

The price you will pay for living paycheck to paycheck is probably the biggest price you will pay in your life. As soon as you can make a different lifestyle happen, do it.

And if you EVER get tempted to live in the Paycheck-to-Paycheck Lifestyle, EVER again in your life, simply come back to this page and read what follows....

The Secret of Motivating Your Self

I was helping a division of a Fortune 500 company recently. (OK, a Fortune 20 company...) Lots of fun and filled with some real "aha" experiences...and some that were almost "aha's".

It generated more fresh ideas in my mind than I've had in a long time. In just a moment I'm going to show you, through story, how to motivate your Self and others with some ideas that were born from the session.

As you read the story, don't forget the message...and then...*record the analysis* for your every day reminder...

You will use an every day reminder in your Daily or Weekly Planner, as part of your Time Plan System later in this book.

The Hamster and the Wheel

Imagine this, because I don't know if it is you...

An individual goes to work five days per week. They "punch in" at 9 and "out" at "5." By an entrepreneur's standards, those are pretty wimpy hours...OK, really wimpy hours. Then it dawned on me that most people who do the "punch in" and "9-5" have to punch in because otherwise no one would know they were there. In other words, it's sort of like wearing an ankle bracelet when you are released from jail and required to be at a certain place at a certain time and nowhere else.

As time passes, the individual becomes like the hamster in the wheel. Each day is like the last and very predictive of the future.

When you say "job", the person immediately thinks of THEIR experience. When you say "work" they think of THEIR OWN "work" or place of employment. After a few months, and then a few years, the person becomes dependent on the job, the company,

...The wheel. It's as if they are a hamster....

Take away the wheel, and the hamster freaks out. "I lost MY job." (Yes the unconscious mind says, "the job that I hate"... the one where they watch the clock to track how many seconds there are until the end of "the day.")

Now, let's move away from this hamster for a moment. Move up a level in thought...

Try and imagine someone coaching the hamster to try a new life. "A new way to create a dream life."

It's almost impossible for the hamster to see anything but the wheel. The wheel is there in the cage and it spins with relative ease. The hamster KNOWS how to do it and doesn't have to THINK ...at all.

The coach starts to work with his hamster client..., "...there is NO hamster wheel over here in this opportunity."

The unconscious mind of the hamster... freaks out!

"What! No wheel?! That's the only thing I know! It's my LIFE! It's what I know how to do and it is what I have mastered...and you want me to go into what looks like a mine field where I will get blown up?!?!?! Someone will come along and TAKE my wheel. They might even ship the wheel to China or Mexico and let another hamster use the wheel and then I will not be able to support my hamsterlets."

Now, the hamster returns to the wheel Monday. Leaving one part of the cage, he hops up onto the wheel and spins for another 8 hours. NOTHING will pry him away from the wheel. NOTHING!

The hamster is annoyed now that there are hamsters in China and Mexico who work the same hours for less money and that they are a threat to stealing his wheel. The hamster, of course, hasn't gone to "Hamster Depot" which is where there are thousands of wheels in all shapes and sizes. In fact, only about 5 out of every 100 hamsters ever goes to Hamsters Depot. When they do, they get nervous, too.

There are SO MANY different wheels to choose from.

Right there, that freaks out even the five brave hamsters. But then something might happen to a couple of the hamsters...They think...that they don't want ANY wheel. Or if they do, they want one that is really cool, provides some value but then look at all the other ways they could use those hours.

These hamsters are a bit different from other hamsters. They decide that they are going to (for some significant time), affiliate with a wheel or two, they are going to go out there and make wheels, mazes, hamster food and all kinds of other things that they will sell to Hamster Depot... instead of punching in and running the wheel for 8 hours.

Of course making wheels and mazes and growing hamster food takes more time, but it is SO MUCH FUN! Hard work? You bet. But those little hamsters work from 9-9 because the line between fun, excitement, adventure and "work" blurs. It's all sort of one thing. Pretty soon they have Mrs. Hamster and their hamsterlets helping with making mazes and wheels and growing hamster food and so on.

The hamsterlets think this is NORMAL....that this life, which is SO different from all the other hamsters in the world, is so cool. They get to go to Hamster Vegas, where there are lots of Hamster Elvis's and other cute hamsters all around that hang out entertaining them. They think: "Isn't that how it is for all hamsters?"

When they go back to their home in Hamster City they find out from their little hamster friends back home that this is **not** the norm.

"Are you kidding, Hamita? My Daddy Hamster is at the wheel all day long and he hates his wheel."

"Why doesn't he just go get a new wheel?" (She doesn't know any different. Everything is evolving in her Hamster Home.)

"It's not that easy, I guess. They get lots of benefits from the wheel."

"What's a benefit?" Hamita retorts.

"I have no idea. I mean, I've never actually seen one. But I'm told that they are really good and VERY important."

"And how long has your Daddy Hamster been there?"

"Since before I was born I think."

"And you have never seen a Hamster Benefit?"

"Well....not really but I am positive that they are important."

...Meanwhile back at Hamster Depot, there are a whole bunch of hamsters outside looking in. The doors are wide open. A few hamsters are actually going in, the doors but most would rather watch with the security of knowing that their wheel is safe and secure. They are curious to be sure. They really admire those that go into Hamster Depot. They wish they could. But they can't ...because...

So now, imagine that you are the hamster's Coach. Now the question is, **how do you get the hamster off the wheel and choose a life that would be rich and fulfilling?** Something the hamster could enjoy and meet all of those life needs and hamster dreams at the same time...or maybe even the dream would be the daily life that the hamster would live. Wouldn't that be cool?

But you can forget it.

It's not going to happen by you telling them anything.

You can tell the hamster that you have a great idea for them, but the fact is that they almost certainly will not get off of their safe, secure, familiar, comfortable yet debilitating wheel. There is too much uncertainty out there in Hamster World.

There is no script to run life off the wheel. There are too many variables in the life you suggest to your Hamster Client..., the ideas you propose, the concepts you describe...unless...

You will fail as the hamster's coach, unless you get the hamster *to voice for himself* the reasons, and more importantly, the feelings of why he absolutely must get off the wheel.

The Epiphany

What happens then is something incredible. An epiphany. When was the last time you suggested something out loud, then verbally said, "No, I can't right now, but I'll think about it for the future"?

Probably never. After all, it is rare to verbally and overtly tell yourself off. You typically don't firmly but politely say, "No thanks, I'm not interested."

Thus...

...leaving Hamster World and coming back to our world....

Ownership of Ideas

If you haven't stumbled across one of the great "Aha's" as to why Time Management before The Time Plan System failed, it was because people didn't take into account other people's ideas, feelings, attitudes and beliefs about THEIR Time Management System.

In other words, even the best intended person can start a time management program and have their life go to pieces because they didn't find out what their boss, their spouse, their kids were thinking about all the changes that would be happening in life!

And by definition, **putting yourself in control of time IS putting yourself in control of your LIFE and your LIFE intersects and overlaps with the people you work with and the people you live with.**

So you'll have to communicate this radical notion of Time Management to those who rely on you and those upon whom you rely.

You must get the person with whom you are communicating to take possession or some ownership of the idea of you designing your life, if you want them to support you and be part of your scheme to have a good life.

There are three basic ways (with lots of subsets) that you can accomplish this outcome.

1. You can ask the person you work or live with to tell you what is important or why they should do what you are proposing.

2. You can ask them to tick off the positive and negative aspects of the proposal and its counter.

3. You can ask them to literally and physically do something as a favor or simply try something, in order to get them to take an action and test the idea.

One way or another it comes down to asking...questions. Discovery. Finding out. Being interested, having empathy.

When you can completely understand what is inside of your fellow hamsters (coworkers, family, and friends) collective heads...then there will be the epiphany. *They see a different world than you do.* And there is absolutely nothing "bad" about thinking like a hamster...after all what else would they think like?

A) What is it like to be inside their head? What are their fears?
B) What are the bad points of their situation?
C) What are the good points of their situation?

They are told that once they get out of Hamster School they must go get a good wheel.

And THAT is the point. In order to have a different, or dream-life to live with you, **the other hamsters must tell you all the reasons that they MUST get rid of the wheel.** They must tell you what they want to find and do out in Hamster World. They must tell you WHY they MUST fill their life with what will make them feel like it all had meaning and purpose.

After all, if you tell them...they will simply jump into their wheel and look over their shoulder to make sure no one takes their wheel and sends it overseas.

If you have them *tell you*, and CONVINCE you, then they'll ship the wheel overseas, themselves.

There are a lot of people who are living in a hamster wheel, and there are a lot of people that aren't. There are a lot of corporations that are great places to hang your hat. And there are many more that aren't.

If you are at one of those wonderful places to be each and every day, you have my ovation. You are fortunate. If you aren't, I'd like to apply for the job of being your Coach. I want you to live the life YOU want to live!

Chapter Two

Finding Your Self in Time: Whose Life Are you Living Anyway?

T he difference between your real self of today...and who you want to be...your **ideal self,** is what is either creating or helping to eliminate a lot of the stress in your life. More importantly, the closer the "self" you want to be (your ideal self) is aligned with the "self" of your actions (the one that's doing stuff today) and your current life, the more fulfilling and juicy is your life.

Question: Are you allowing your ideal self to suffer?

You've lived a life to date that has brought you to where you are. A very good thing, maybe. But there is time in life left to do what you want and live the life you DESIRE and DREAM. It is absolutely time to step into the future and do the following exercises.

The First Future: No change

Briefly imagine that you are not going to live and discover your unfulfilled dreams. Instead, you continue doing what you have in the past. What will life be like in 10 years?

It will be just like today; with one difference...you will have 10 fewer years remaining in your life. I want you to think about how you will feel in 10 years if you continue to do the exact same things you have to date. What will your daily life be like?

The Ideal Future: Your Design

Now, imagine that you are 10 years into your future but this time it's different. Why? Because starting TODAY you actually begin making the changes you want in your life. Of course, **just because you want these specific and intentional changes doesn't mean they are easy to implement.** They are intentional because these changes are the changes that YOU are choosing and they are the changes that will CAUSE you to live the life YOU want to live and dream. *YOUR CHOICES and DECISIONS often mean leaving the perception of security in order to discover your own personal freedom and what that means.*

Just go there now. 10 years out, having made a decade of changes. Imagine living the life you WANT to live. How does that feel inside? Do you feel that you have LIVED life?!

All of this sounds right and feels like it makes sense, but, *HOW* do you do this?! *HOW* do you actually make all the changes necessary to live a life that you create?

How do you know WHAT changes will bring about the life you want? How can you be sure? What is the syntax (the exact sequence of events) that will take you to where you want to be? This is an exhilarating exercise. You need to do this now:

1. **Dedicate a sturdy journal, notebook or create a document on your computer for this exercise.** Write without stopping. Fill in the blanks for this sentence: **"3 years from now, I plan to be living in a ...at...with..."** Get really detailed about it. You do this because you are hooking up neural connections in your mind in a way you never have. THEN you must begin to revisit this "document" every day, read it and revise it. You must improve upon, clarify and make clear just exactly who and what you are going to be doing, experiencing, living and having in 3 years. This is the first step of the process!

KEYPOINT: Notice how you felt excited and optimistic when you did this? The reason is simple. It's the life YOU are designing instead of the one that was given to you and that you have been living with less intention and purpose, until now.

If you don't do this exercise, you can forget the rest of this book. This is YOUR LIFE you are creating, not an omelet. Get detailed, be precise and literally design like an artist or an architect...for that is precisely what you are doing! Spend at least a half hour today on this, and then continue.

2. To truly LIVE the LIFE you want to live, it's going to have to be more than about having money, though that is obviously important. Life is bigger than stuff. **Write down some guiding values and principles that guide your life TODAY and that you want to KEEP for the future.** ["I try and be helpful to others"; "I believe the word 'nice' is a cool word"; "I believe that being authentic beats all other options".] You may also want to write some specific guiding principles for the future that you haven't had in place to date. In other words, what kinds of attitudes and values do you want to be important to you from today forward? *The key element here is to be certain that these are YOUR values and principles, and* ***not someone else's****!* These will be important drivers going forward and obviously you'll revisit this again and again.

3. **Finally, I want you to write a Quick List of 20-25 things you want to experience in the next 3 years.** I call this a *Get To Do List!* Some of these things might be experiences you've had in the past, but for the most part, focus on **new experiences that will be the rewards of your new life**. These can be things you will have, do or be. They might be travel objectives, books you want to write, music you want to record, the house you want to build, the family you want to parent, the changes in your life you want to make.

*Keep this list near you every day. Update it and revise the list monthly...but review the document in detail **every day.*** This is the beginning. This is the genesis of creating the life you want to live. If you were to purchase a property and build a home, you would definitely have an architect design the house for you before the builder laid the foundation. No one can build a house without a plan! For the most part, we live the life that has been planned for us. It's now time to take the drafting tools in hand and do it yourself!

When you have determined where you want your life to be in one year – or five, it will have an impact on what you do TODAY. A person who dreams of being a lawyer will not have much success obtaining that goal if they don't first make the time to fit studying and school into their schedule today.

KEYPOINT: If you are finally attempting to be in charge of your time, it is because you recognize that there is a limited supply and time is valuable.

Many longer-term goals will have short-term goals that lead directly to them. Not only does this make practical sense (i.e.: getting accepted to University is a shorter term goal than becoming a partner in a law firm) but it also helps you from becoming overwhelmed or losing sight of your goals.

While responsibilities at work and home may be what dictate how you plan your day, shouldn't all (or most) of this time work in harmony with your goals?

This may mean some big changes, or it may just mean adjusting some things in your routine. When you start planning your time with a goal in mind, it is easier to appreciate the benefits of what you are doing and prevents you from getting caught up in time wasters – activities that use up your time but are ultimately unprofitable either in money or your personal life.

My outcome in this book is to help you recognize and drill deep into the inner reaches of your mind all of these facts and realities, so you can create different plans with a different thinking process than before having read this book. My next outcome is to let you see the problems in advance, so you have long prepared for them weeks, months or years before they come to pass. My next outcome is to eradicate those things within your control that block you from leading your best and most ideal life…and most especially to stop procrastination.

I am going to show you how to set goals that WILL be achieved and that will be motivating enough so that when your SELF REGULATION tank gets close to empty toward the last half or third of the day, you have already accomplished the most important things in your life, for your life.

Finally, I want to let you in on the secrets of productivity. For when we are productive in the areas of life that are important to us, whatever those are, life takes on more significance and meaning.

And to bring all of this together is a new way of looking at life, a new view on "managing" time, which we'll call Time Management, but is better recognized as a Time Plan. Much as the airplane needs a flight plan, your daily life needs a Time Plan.

And it is within these pages that you will begin to see all of this come together for you!

Chapter Three

Your Life...Your Time

Y ou made it this far, so you didn't get scared by the notion of change. That puts you in the top 20%.

You can think of Time as a currency, because it is.

You can think of Money as a currency, because it is.

"Time is money." That of course is not true. Time can be exchanged for money. There IS equivalence.

10 hours of your time doing yard work is worth $X

10 hours of your time doing whatever it is you are good at is worth perhaps, $5X

Time and money can be exchanged for each other.

Sex is often exchanged for money as well, legally, illegally, implied or explicit. This of course is true. Many people say, "She married him for his money." And that of course is probably true. And perhaps he married her because she was beautiful, which approaches the notion that sex can be exchanged for money.

I bring this up, not only to keep you on your toes, but also to point out that sex is often part of love. Love is a complex concept that goes far beyond the scope of this book. I will promise you this: If you don't give people your time, they will fall out of love with you. They might still hold you dear but the value on that love, the intensity, will not be as great.

So is the equation:

Time = Money = Sex

Is that true? Absolutely not. However they often can be exchanged for each other in varying amounts. The common thread of (almost) every human that lives today is that sex brought them into this world. Yet the one thing I never see on people's Goal Lists, or "Get To Do List" is "have sex." Why?

Here is the first rule of using your time and getting what you want in life: Be honest with yourself so you can be REAL with other people. Know what you *really* want in life and be able to say so. Now, I don't see "Love" on a lot of Goal Lists either. I coach people from all over the world and I have to cajole them into telling me why Sex didn't make their Top 25 things...then after some probing I find out that it's really in their Top 5 and often #1.

I'll say it first. I am good at Time Management and probably the most productive human I "know," in large part because I love sex and I love . . . love.

One of the key factors of causing more time to be available in the future was the subject of a new study at UCLA.

Key Points:

1. **Money challenges are easier to anticipate** because money is more tangible than time. Money problems are recurring and people know that they will need to have significant changes in their life if they are ever to have money.

2. **People predict they will have lots of time in the future for things they like** but are unaware that their predictions are off the mark because they have neglected to take into consideration several key factors in their "thinking process."

3. Because people assume they will have enough time in the future, not needing substantial paradigm shifts and behavioral changes that they over commit themselves today for tomorrow, **assuring a life that gets more stressful** as each day progresses.

4. **Having more time and money is not a time management issue**...it is much more complex than that simple task. Why? Because every day life happens; and it's very difficult to prepare for life without a truly powerful plan.

If your appointment book runneth over, it could mean one of two things: Either you are enviably popular, or you make the same faulty assumptions about the future as everyone else.

Psychological research points to the latter explanation. Research by two business school professors reveals that people over-commit because **we expect to have more time in the future than we have in the present**. Of course, when tomorrow turns into today, we discover that we are too busy to do everything we promised.

Gal Zauberman, PhD, of the University of North Carolina at Chapel Hill, and John Lynch Jr., PhD, of Duke University, learned some fascinating tidbits about time, money and the future using paper-and-pencil questionnaires (respondents to seven different surveys numbered 95, 68, 241, 61, 264, 48 and 130) that that this expectation of more time "slack," a surplus of a given resource available to complete a task, is more pronounced for time than money. The authors suspect that's because every day's a little different: The nature of time fools us and we "forget" about how things fill our days. Money is more "fungible," freely exchanged for something of like kind -- such as four quarters for a dollar bill.

Write Zauberman and Lynch, "Barring some change in employment or family status, supply and demand of money are relatively constant over time, and people are aware of that. Compared with demands on one's time, money needs in the future are relatively predictable from money needs today."

Participants believed that both **time and money would be more available in "a month" than "today,"** and believed it **more strongly for time than for money**.

A deeper investigation of a psychological phenomenon called "delay discounting," in **which people tend to lessen the importance of future rewards**, showed that people also **discounted future time more than both gains and losses in future money**.

Zauberman and Lynch continue, "People are consistently surprised to be so busy today. Lacking knowledge of what specific tasks will compete for their time in the future, they **act as if new demands will not inevitably arise that are as pressing as those faced today**."

In short, the future is ideal: The fridge is stocked, the weather clear, the train runs on schedule and meetings end on time. Today, well, stuff happens. To crosscheck support for their hypotheses, the authors ran a final survey that measured the expected growth or contraction of slack time and slack money over time. They tested how those expectations predicted subsequent decisions to invest time or money at two points in time. As before, participants who expected to have more time but not more money discounted future time investments more than they discounted future money investments. Participants who expected to have more money than time showed a mirror-image pattern. Say the authors, "This is important because it demonstrates that the resource dependency we observed in the earlier experiments is explainable by changes in slack."

Can people learn to predict future time demands that are more in line with reality? The authors observe, "It is difficult to learn from feedback that time will not be more abundant in the future. Specific activities vary from day to day, so people do not learn from feedback that, in aggregate, total demands are similar." Money's "slack pools" are smoother, more equal and more predictable over time.

Chapter Four

To Live Life YOUR WAY, You End Procrastination

W ill You Procrastinate or Not?
So I've said I want more "free time," more money, more time for love, and more sex.

That's where I'm at right now. How about you? Managing time well is what gives you and I more of what we want and helps us get rid of those things we don't want. If I want more F,M,L, and S then I have to be willing to knock some stuff out of my daily life. There are after all only 24....

But even though you are pretty clear about what you want, you are almost guaranteed to procrastinate. I confess that I used to procrastinate...a lot. That's not true today, but I had to find out a lot of answers to burn that bridge. So if I want more F, M, L and S will I procrastinate? How about you? Let's find out...

Here are a few scenarios where people will almost certainly procrastinate and a few where they won't. See if you can guess which is which.

- You've asked me to help you build up the courage to ask someone out/to dance, whatever. You and I walk into the club/bar and I sit down, have a glass of wine and tell you to go for it, motioning my hand at the vast array of fish in the sea here for the sole purpose of being asked out. "Go for it, check in with me before you leave."

Procrastinate or not?

- You've asked me to help you get a job. I have asked you numerous questions and you have responded as to what your talents, likes, dislikes are. I tell you that based on the information you've given me, "I want you to go apply at X, Y and Z companies for job Q and I want you to go, in that order, reporting back at 5 PM."

Will you procrastinate or not?

- You've asked me to help you launch your small coffee table business so you can actually start to build a nest egg. I speak in an upbeat motivational fashion to you and tell you that you have the courage, the power, the strength, and that you can do it. I show you how crucial it is for you to have a small little "You INC." I lay it out that you will literally build wealth if you will just do this one thing. "Now find something that you love and do it."

Throughout this book I **will encourage you to have a "small Coffee Table Business."** What is that? It's a business that you run from your Coffee Table! A 1 or 2 or 3 person "business," which provides you with income and tax benefits that will be fun or interesting or filled with meaning.

I teach people how to build a business on the Internet. The rent is cheap. The help is cheap. The job security is guaranteed. The work is fascinating and there is nothing that is hard. It's work but you end up earning money while you sleep and waking up with money in your mailbox. (There's a lot to be said for that!)

Until then, will you procrastinate or not?

New Research Reveals a Key Procrastination Factor

First study: (All performed by Dr. Sean McCrea at the University of Konstanz in Germany) Half of the students in a study are asked to write about why someone might want to open a bank account or keep a diary.

The other half was asked to write a couple of sentences about how they would open a bank account or keep a diary.

After this was done, half the students in a new study were asked to provide examples of members of a group, for example, naming types of birds.

The other half of the students was instructed to name the type of category to which birds belonged.

Third and final study: All the students in this study were given money and a time limit to examine a copy of "La Parade" by the 19th century artist Georges Seurat. 1/2 was then given information about "pointillism." (The technique Seurat used to make colors that appeared solid from small dots like pixels). The other 1/2 was told that the painting was an example of neo-impressionism in which the author had used color to evoke harmony and emotion.

KEYPOINT: How you frame a project or task in your mind is going to, in large part, determine whether you will even BEGIN the task. Concrete terms? You'll almost certainly do it. Abstract? It's a coin flip.

Both groups were then asked to rate the importance of color in 13 other works of art. *Psychological Science* reported the findings. The results were striking. What did the researchers find   out?

Almost ALL students given tasks in CONCRETE TERMS completed their assignments in each study.

About HALF of the students asked to think in abstract terms didn't even RESPOND to the questions/tasks, which they were PAID to do.

A person asked to go find someone and ask him or her out is daunting. Walking up to a singular person with the instruction to ask THAT person out is not as freezing.

Telling someone to go apply for a job at X, Y and Z for position Q is much more effective than telling someone the economy is terrible and they better get moving before they fall through the ceiling too.

And the Coffee Table business? Yes, you need it to build wealth, but if I don't tell you what to do (if I let you be a "free" and thinking human) you probably won't do it. If I tell you to sell collectibles that you can buy from ABC store and drop ship to customers on Ebay, you'll almost certainly begin.

If this is the kind of valuable information you need to know, something you've wondered about, and been bugged about...wondering why you don't do things you know you should...or wondering why THEY don't do what you "tell them."
Identify the person's (your own!) negative behavior and give a

SPECIFIC and CONCRETE instruction as to what to do instead. Whether people say "yes" or "no" (or don't ever think about it again). I will help you eliminate procrastination by being concrete with you in this book, if you will eliminate procrastination today.

KEYPOINT: Like so many other problems, procrastination is not THE problem but a reaction to other problems that creates a domino effect. When you procrastinate, you are trying to SOLVE another problem.

The Central Reason you picked up this book is because you are like anyone else. You procrastinate and you don't want to. So, how do you know if you will? How do you know if you will actually set goals that can be accomplished without self-sabotaging along the way? As you're discovering, there's lots and lots of reasons that goal setting and getting a life of your own, can go awry. **There are lots of reasons you don't take an action when you** *want to take an action!*

Dr. Piers Steel recently reported on his discovery of the Procrastination Equation. Steel identifies four different factors in addition to lack of concrete thinking.

The Simple Formula for Predicting Procrastination

Will you Do IT or will you Procrastinate? Here's the formula that will give you the answer. (Did you hate math? Don't worry, no test coming.) There are four factors in Steel's formula to predict procrastination.

EV/DI or more simply.... (ExV) divided by (DxI)

Expectation X Value / Deadline X Individual Sensitivity

With that in mind, here are the elements of the Formula:

Factor 1: (E)xpectation of Success

Can you actually pull it off? Can you really DO the task in the first place? Or is it just out of your league or your belief structure. If you don't think you have the ability or skills, or if the task is just too big, too daunting, then you will almost certainly procrastinate, right?

This notion of *competence* is very important in the procrastination decision. If you don't perceive yourself as *capable*, it isn't going to get done, because you feel like you will fail and people just won't tackle things that believe they will fail at. This is very, very sad, because, in order to reach ANY GOAL it will require failure en route...and probably a lot of failure.

The more competent you feel you are, the less likely you are to procrastinate.

Factor 2: The (V)alue of Completing the Task

The value of getting taxes done is your personal freedom.

This "voluntary act" assures that you will stay out of jail. The value of finishing feeding the baby is huge. The baby will be calm and allow your sanity to return and heart rate to slow down. But you may not feel the value of promoting and marketing your new website to the world. After all part of you believes that people should just come. The lower the value your mind places on the task, the greater the likelihood you will procrastinate. It's that simple.

The more valuable or important the project is to you, the less like you are to procrastinate!

Factor 3: The Task (D)eadline or, Just How Soon Does This Have to Be Done?

You must determine, "Does it REALLY have to be done, or is it just a WANT?"

You must do your taxes by the deadline or there is punishment attached that is greater than by not doing them. You just can't let taxes slide. So the April 15 deadline is very real and you will make sure your taxes are done before that. However, they don't have to be done before that date, at least not by much.

And the baby could be crying and the baby is as demanding for food and change as the government is for your money. But the baby is louder and the punishment for not doing so is more severe than not doing your taxes yet. So you change the baby first. It has to be done just as fast as you want to be out of pain.

There are deadlines at work of varying magnitude and closeness in time. The closer the time, the more likely the person will not procrastinate on the issue. The further in time away from this very moment, the more likely the person will procrastinate.

The critical factor of deadline and absolute requirement of completion increase the probability you will not procrastinate and you will get it done.

Factor 4: The (I)ndividual's Sensitivity to the Desirability of the Task

Your brain is like anyone else's. The brain resists doing that which it doesn't like, enjoy, etc. etc. And that is MOST EVERYTHING. So the first factor is really simple: **If you desire the task, it becomes much more likely you will Do the task and not procrastinate.**

Do you find it desirable or undesirable and to what degree or magnitude? I don't like doing taxes (-10) more than I don't like cutting the lawn (-6) which I don't like more than media interviews (-3). And there is the positive side, the positive numbers.

I'd much rather enjoy sex (+10) than see a fun show in Las Vegas (+7). I'd much rather see a fun show in Las Vegas than play cards (+6) and I'd much rather play cards than do a keynote (+5) which is more desirable than doing a full day training (+4) which I do enjoy, just not as much as sex, which is more desirable than taking a walk in the fresh air (+3).

So faced with doing taxes or having ...you can see the -10 vs. potentially +10 right? Your brain does instant calculations that will in quick time create decisions conscious and non-conscious.

In sum, the four factors of the Simple Procrastination Formula are:

- Expectation of Success *(Can I do it/do it well?)*
- Value of Completing the Task *(How important is it to me to finish?)*
- Deadline of Task *(How soon does it have to be done?)*
- Individual Sensitivity to Task *(How much don't I like this?)*

Those are the four key factors that predict procrastination...and it turns out, a whole lot more.

Before I close this section, the procrastination research that yielded the formula came up with a few tendencies worth thinking about as you work on goal setting, productivity and time management.

- Procrastinators are **low in self-confidence**
- Perfectionists procrastinate **less** than others, but worry about it more
- 15-20% of the general public are *chronic procrastinators*!
- Procrastinators tend to **fail to plan** retirement or pay taxes, two disaster scenarios
- "Whether you believe you can or can't, you're probably right," is often true with procrastinators
- As self-control increases, our **expectancy** about resisting temptation follows.

These aren't the only four factors in procrastination but more than any, they help you predict whether you are inclined to procrastinate on this project, or not. Knowing that it's going to rain is a helpful piece of information. Knowing a hurricane is going to hit in 3 days and it's going to wipe out the entire area...is important information.

But just *knowing* what is likely to happen, or even knowing what WILL happen in no way assures you that your brain will allow your conscious mind free will to deal with the issue. Your brain is comfortable living in this house and it doesn't wrap it's mind around what a hurricane is, and even after it rips an area to shreds, killing many people, it STILL doesn't mean you will do ANYTHING in your best interest if it hasn't faced this situation regularly in the past (and by past I also mean back in Caveman days).

In other words, the formula predicts the weather, but it doesn't cause us to do the right or smart thing. It just predicts.

Chapter Five

Procrastination's Voice

R unning your life and managing your time SHOULD be easy. You know you're supposed to cut the lawn or clean the house today...and you don't. Part of you just didn't feel up to it. If you can't get all of your "parts" to agree with "you" then you will simply never stop procrastinating. Nothing complicated about it.

When people say, "a part of me just feels" or "part of me wants to and "part of me doesn't"...that's pretty common place phrasing in hypnotherapy. It is true, but it is also a metaphor. There are no parts or people in the brain...it just seems that way.

In this chapter I want to refer to three hypothetical and different "parts" of you in a rather sarcastic and slightly playful way. Play along and you'll know when it all sinks in...

If you want to understand why you procrastinate, you must first look beyond the ancient concept that laziness alone is the root of procrastination. If it were, procrastination would be easy to eliminate...but....of course...it's more complicated than that...You are not TRYING to create a problem. Your problem may be that you are afraid to take on that new project for fear of failure, or that you fear success and attention and feel you are not worthy of that attention, or that you feel you will not do a good job and everyone will judge you harshly.

At the non-conscious level, these drivers of procrastination are forms of self-sabotage, and I'll come back to that later. The fact is, there are many reasons why people procrastinate and those reasons may change depending on the person and the situation. Sometimes it's hard to figure out WHY you are procrastinating. But, if you just step back and start analyzing your procrastination, you'll find this is worthwhile, even if it is hard to come up with any answers in the beginning. Eventually, this self-introspection and analysis will pay off!

Getting to Know the "Personality" of Your Conscious Mind

Ask yourself about "the personality of your Conscious Mind." You know, the part of you that says, "What the heck was I thinking?" Exactly who are those little guys and girls who stand on your shoulder and remind you what you should be doing and judge you when you do NOT do what you should? Here are a few of countless possibilities:

Mr. Zen

Mr. Zen got eaten by the lion when it was his turn to stand guard in front of the Cave two million years ago. Nevertheless, Mr. Zen evolved because he is **where the body wants to be.** Out of fear, out of danger and in the moment either sleeping, snoozing, resting or partaking in some addictive pleasures.

This guy allows you to "be in the moment." Mr. Zen denies the reality of your procrastination, blaming it on others or telling you that it isn't such a big deal to miss a deadline. "Don't stress out over it." *Slurp.*

> **KEYPOINT: Focus on the very real fact that you tend to ignore projects and tasks and seek pleasure instead, and it can only lead to being a pawn in someone else's life....and...** *Slurp.*

If this is a "big part of you," you aren't likely to respond to the repeated signals to change, unless something really bad happens. You might fail a class or get fired, or lose a relationship because of your failure to fulfill promises and complete tasks. Before this happens to you, you want to find a way to put enough leverage on your Self and get your life moving!

Stop kidding yourself by thinking it is OK to blow off work or obligations and commitments just so you can have a good time. There are plenty of times when it is more than OK to be in the moment. In fact, it can be great to be in the moment. BUT, if you are there, making plans and decisions only as life happens you become a pleasure stimulus addict. (Take your pick: Drugs, alcohol, cigarettes, whatever.)

Decide now: Take complete responsibility for your obligations and for your future, and focus on what YOU DECIDE YOU WANT in life, or, you will never amount to anything, and you are likely to lose friends, family, jobs and opportunities in the process. Never give up enjoyable things, but allow yourself to plan for more of those moments and do fewer in the moment so you can feed your kids…today and tomorrow!

Mr. Critic

Mr. Critic can be cruel, mean-spirited and hypercritical both of others and your Self. It might be telling you that you will fail, that you are not capable of achieving your potential.

> **KEYPOINT: Don't LISTEN to every muttering of your barely conscious parts of your SELF. Get the project done, AND THEN listen to your SELF.**

Sending these mixed signals only results in one thing: you become frozen in place and do not start or continue with what you want to accomplish. You may create your own life-obstacles by telling yourself that you will hate the task and you will be miserable while you are working on the task, or by saying that the task is stupid and you shouldn't have to do it, and feeling victimized.

Answer: Too bad.

File the lawsuit later.

OR, you may tell yourself that you will ONLY work on the task if you are guaranteed that the results will be perfect, or that you will get paid. (Always try to avoid thinking you might be God. He has no need for the lousy company or competition. Do a good job. A really good job and get ON with it.) OR perhaps you will stop a project because you think you are going to fail miserably - all the while telling yourself you really need to get this done and stop procrastinating!

MORE IMPORTANT: First and foremost, you need to put attention on your self-esteem and confidence.

Confidence usually comes from having seen your Self having done something well. ***Competence breeds confidence***. But when you haven't done something before, you have very little competence. Fair enough.

Now it's time to believe in your SELF. Allow your Self to KNOW that YOU are a COMPETENT PERSON and that you can accomplish most anything you want, albeit there will be plenty of screw ups, pain, and frustration along the way. Got it?

Excellent. While we're here . . .

You also must take a look at life and ask yourself why you think that everything you do must be fun and pleasant. It isn't...it isn't going to be and any hallucination pointed in this direction is a big self-sabotage bomb waiting to go off.

Mr. Chaos

This voice really wants you to do your best and may try to help you achieve your goal, but it is disorganized and lacks the skill. If you never learned how to organize and manage your time, you may find it hard to get things done, even if the voice on your shoulder is telling you that you should.

I watch people live in chaos. They have TONS of time but have no plan. Maybe they were rewarded for putting things off in the past - maybe their parents always found an excuse for their behavior and told them it was OK, or someone picked up the task and completed it for them to cover for their failure.

If this is you, tell your friends and family not to cover for you or do your work for you. In fact, **tell them what YOU are going to DO and to keep the pressure ON YOU until it's DONE. Take total responsibility for the things you do not finish on time or the things you do that are not done well.**

Everyone's non-conscious self has his or her own way of "escape." This way allows the procrastinator to justify and explain away the procrastination. It may be fear, the need for excitement and entertainment, resentment over having to work on a task, manipulation or irrational expectations about how long something may take or how difficult it will be to accomplish.

And of course...we only talked about three valences of procrastination...but enough to get the idea!

KEYPOINT: Once you've come out of the "closet" as a procrastinator, you can only continue to procrastinate if you spin the outcome of your procrastination in a positive light.

Now, look at different manifestations of what happens when you procrastinate:

- Optimism about how long the project will take and how hard it will be to complete. It won't be hard, and it won't take that long so, therefore, I don't have to start NOW.

- Sudden panic as you realize that you are really behind schedule and you have to make up for lost time. (The Stress Response for being disorganized and having no plan or preparedness.)

- Motivation to work on a task at the last minute because you have been backed into a corner, all the while resenting your loss of freedom and the idea that you were forced to accomplish this project. (Get over this!)

Think about the things that may be at the root of each of these issues. How many of these apply to you?

- **Self Esteem** - You struggle with feelings of incompetence, and poor self-esteem. (All but the narcissist struggle with feelings of incompetence at some time or another.)

- You insist on a high level or an extremely high **standard** of performance though you feel you are incapable of achieving this performance.
- **Pressure** - You use procrastination to deal with the pressure of daily life and all the competing obligations and tasks.
- You know that if you get this project done, someone will just give you **another** project to do. And the gal in the cubicle next door gets paid the very same to do less. (Welcome to government mentality.)
- **Control** - You use procrastination as a means of control. You don't like to be pushed around and you feel that you should decide what to do and when to perform the task. You'll do what you want to, when you want to.
- **Justification** - You feel that others do not understand how busy you are and how complicated your life is. It isn't that you procrastinate - it's just that others don't understand your problems.
- You often feel like a **victim** and you are frustrated that others don't see how unfair it is.

The more often you procrastinate, the more you reinforce the behavior, and the harder it is to interrupt the cycle. You screw yourself in and get in so tight you can't get out.

For every project on which you procrastinate, you reinforce:

Inaction.... instead of... *Action*
Avoidance... instead of... *Proactive Participation*
Current State... instead of... *Desired State*
Fear... instead of... *Confidence*

Consider the following examples of classic roots of procrastination:

Issue: Motivation

Problem: You feel this project is irrelevant and has no meaning for you.

Solution: Find a way to make this project more interesting, delegate it to someone else if that is appropriate OR negotiate a reward or result with the person who assigned the task.

Issue: Competence/Training

Problem: You feel you do not have the training or knowledge to accomplish this project, or you are uncertain about taking on something you have not done before.

Solution: Be sure you fully understand the outcome everyone expects. If you need help, get support, advice, guidance or training from someone who is expert or better educated in this area.

Issue: Standards

Problem: You are afraid you will not perform on the project perfectly.

Solution: Analyze just how important the project is and determine how Mr. Critic is over-striving for perfection. Consider what you would expect of a friend, or co-worker if they were performing on the project. Is perfection necessary, or even possible?

Issue: Obligations

Problem: You may not be able to fulfill all of your obligations because you have so much to do.

Solution: Try to renegotiate deadlines or schedules so that you can prioritize your tasks and get everything done on time.

Issue: Assumptions

Problem: You believe that if you avoid or ignore the project it will evaporate. You assume that it will take less time or effort to accomplish.

Solution: Accept that the project must be accomplished and establish a written plan to 'chunk' the items into smaller pieces with logical milestones to progress toward the end goal. Put reasonable times to each of these points in time and then revaluate the timeline for completing the entire task.

Issue: Fear

Problem: You are worried about how others may evaluate or judge you.

Solution: Consider the true impact on your life. Will this task really be so important that others will scrutinize the outcome and are they really likely to care all that much about the results and judge you harshly?

Issue: Avoidance

Problem: You just hate doing this kind of stuff.
Solution: Can you find a way to make it tolerable or give yourself a reward when you have completed the task to give you something to which you can look forward? Do it before anything else and just get it out of the way.

Circle the issues above that you feel apply to you and use them later for your Personal Plan to Prevent Procrastination!

What do you see as the 'root' of your most common manifestations of procrastination?

- **Self Worth** - If you constantly downplay your skills and knowledge and doubt your own ability you will

THEN, defuse the voice - silence it by changing your mindset. The way you think and the things you tell yourself will, over time, have a positive effect on old habits.

Mr. Zen

This state of mind is the child who wants only to do what THEY want to do and insists on distracting you from other tasks by thinking of things to do that are more pleasant.

This voice will tell you that there is no real problem with putting off the task. It will get done - all in good time! The Mr. Zen voice is easy to listen to because he allows you to avoid the things you really don't feel like doing, or the things about which you are uncertain, or the things you don't LIKE to do.

You can quiet this voice by telling your Self that you will have plenty of time to enjoy what you want to do. Literally PLAN an event to take place after the completion date of the task to reward yourself.

Don't forget to remind yourself that there is a different kind of satisfaction in achieving a goal, even if the work itself is not engaging or fun. You may be making someone else happy, or advancing yourself toward a longer-term goal, which will make you VERY happy when you get there.

Recognizing small milestones will give you more confidence and remind you that you are achieving something, and it will keep the Mr. Zen voice quieter.

Mr. Critic

This state of mind finds you inferior in every way. If you DO accomplish a task, this Mr. Critic will tell you that if it isn't perfect, it isn't good enough. If you DON'T accomplish a task, Mr. Critic will tell you that you never get anything done and that you really need to get yourself together!

This voice speaks to your low self-worth and your uncertainty. It makes you wonder if you can accomplish the thing you are trying to make yourself do and pretty soon you are frozen and cannot move! You can calm this voice by setting near-term goals and congratulating yourself and recognizing your achievements as you accomplish your milestones. AND, you can quiet that Mr. Critic by reminding yourself that everything does not have to be perfect to be 'well done' and that trying your best is all you can do.

You should also remind your Self (and Mr. Critic) that you don't have to think so far out into the future to imagine the worst.

Instead, all you have to do is to START the task and keep going, one step at a time. The future will take care of itself! Fend off the voice of doom by keeping tasks and outcomes in perspective. Remind yourself that even if the task isn't a complete success, it will be better than total failure or not even TRYING to do it and you will learn from the experience. Focus on your strengths and skills and silence Mr. Critic!

Mr. Chaos

Chaotic procrastination is rooted mostly in the absence of organizational skills, which can easily be learned. Of course you'll have to practice, and it will take time to break the bad habits, but you can accomplish this with a little effort. The Mr. Chaos voice is trying very hard to help you start and finish projects but this voice just doesn't have the information you need to get the job done!

The planning and time management processes you acquire will give you the ability to establish a calendar with milestones. You can organize your work in such a way that you create 'chunks' of tasks to accomplish; all focused toward meeting your longer-term goal. A large part of these processes involves things like 'Action Lists', 'To Do Lists', and writing goals and objectives for longer-term things, like becoming President of a company, or completing your degree by a certain date.

Strengthen your attention span by starting a project and focusing on the task for a half an hour. Then give yourself a 15-minute break. When the 15 minutes is finished, go back to work. Keep doing this (you can set a timer or alarm if that helps) until you gradually extend your ability to concentrate on a project and stay on target for several hours, with a small break every 2 hours or so. The Mr. Chaos voice is often heard by that part of you that just doesn't know where to begin - the part that gets easily overwhelmed and frustrated.

If you have a plan for small steps, and if you prove to yourself that you can focus on structured tasks for a reasonable period of time, you will begin to quiet the voice of chaos. Now that you have considered the issues, the root of these issues and the techniques you can use to soothe the voices on your shoulder, you can begin to sketch out some details, as a first step toward...

Making your Personal Plan to Prevent Procrastination

Using a Journal that you can keep and use for years to come, complete the information below. You will use it later for your Personal Plan!

For the purpose of this exercise, choose **ONE** task or activity you are currently putting off and describe it. (Did you paint the deck? Did you write the book? Did you get the car fixed? Did you...?)

On the next page, list up to five reasons (or feelings) you believe you are delaying that one task or activity.

Then, for each reason you are delaying the activity or task, come up with a solution (a reason you SHOULD work on the task that will silence the issues that have caused you to procrastinate).

Task I'm Putting Off:

Why I Believe I'm Putting This Off:

1)

2)

3)

4)

5)

Solutions:

1)

2)

3)

4)

5)

Create an action plan with the major steps and activities, and associated dates, to get you to your goal of completing the task. These don't have to be detailed, but they should contain enough information to remind you of what needs to be done in each step. Use a separate sheet of paper, if you need to list more activities/dates or details.

Start Date_____

Activity 1:

Date_____

Activity 2:

Date_____

Activity 3:

Date_____

Activity 4:

Date_____

Activity 5:

Date_____

End Date_____

Use this **ONE** task and your plan to complete that task as a 'test plan'. As you pursue your goal, write down thoughts and issues you encounter, and figure out how you are going to address these obstacles or issues when you tackle the next task.

Procrastination: Practicing for Death?

When people excel at procrastination I sometimes gently remind them that they are doing an excellent job at preparing for death. Think about it. Make sense?

You know so many people who will never earn more for their family than they are today but just can't pull the trigger at either:

A) Starting an easy home style business that would add significantly to their bottom line or,

B) Finishing projects that they've started.

And of course when you procrastinate, nothing can work...because nothing is begun, continued or finished. "It" does NOT work. "IT" never does. You and only you, decide if IT will work.

Here's the thing: **The car does not go to a gas station by itself and fill up with gasoline. But EVERY TIME YOU go to the gas station you fill the car up with gasoline.** There is no "wondering" if IT will work.

I never wonder if "IT" will sell or "IT" will work. It won't. IT never does. Either I choose it to happen or I don't. And that's just one glaring example.

Our Internet web site shouldn't make the kind of money "it" generates. I can tell you a dozen reasons why, but the fact is, that IT doesn't generate money. I decide if it will and I put my attention there and THEN it does. There is no question about the result.

Most people who procrastinate don't get things done once they start them...most people are pretty honest with themselves and recognize it. But it can really be helpful to quantify a future-threatening problem like procrastination. That's the purpose of this questionnaire you get to do now. A questionnaire is obviously not a scientific instrument. What this questionnaire does is allow you to take a snapshot of yourself as far as putting off important things in life. It brings to consciousness possible future triggers that will save you a wasted week.

There is no personality disorder or disease that goes along with a high or low score. But don't be surprised if there is a diagnosis by 2020 for procrastination because THEN it will be able to be treated and generate revenue…all that for another day….

This glimpse inside of yourself simply helps you find where you can trigger more positive behaviors…and like all good questionnaires, there is a self-scoring tool that should be used with the understanding it is a little more accurate than a horoscope.

If you find the guide conflicts with how you see yourself, then start logging in your journal each day what you wanted to be doing when you made your plan for the day, and contrast it with what really happened. If you want to cheat and get a "perfect score," just check the right hand column all the way down. If you want to be a procrastination martyr just check all the things under "often!" (Remember this isn't a test. No one sees this. Honest self-examination is free of charge and causes no pain you haven't felt already.)

OK, let's get to it.

The Procrastination Questionnaire

Often (4)   Sometimes (3)   Rarely (2) or Never (1)

1. When I am working on a task, I start thinking about something else or I begin to daydream.

2. I tend to focus on instant gratification that satisfies me rather than my goals.

3. When I anticipate the worst it stops me in the tracks and demotivates me.

4. I sell or represent a product or company that is of questionable reputation...leaving me to wonder if what I'm selling is the right thing to do.

5. I find it hard to concentrate for long periods of time.

6. I do things that I think need to be done whether they are the things that I have been asked or told to do nor not.

7. If I have a problem that I can't get out of my head, it distracts me from other tasks.

8. I put off things I really don't feel like doing or things I think may be difficult.

9. I waste a lot of time.

10. I daydream about grand success, but I don't see any progress.

11. I act without thinking when there is a crisis or problem.

12. I delay tasks until it is nearly too late to get them completed.

13. I miss deadlines and fail to get things done - even if they are important to my success.

14. I can't get interested in anything unless it is entertaining, exciting or enjoyable.

15. I put off tasks I don't like until my well being is threatened or damaged.

16. I make no significant progress toward my goals on most days.

17. I find myself doing one thing when I know I should be concentrating on something else - but I can't help myself.

18. I am easily distracted by something I find entertaining or enjoyable.

19. If I don't feel like doing something, I find an excuse not to do it.

20. I get anxious if I feel something is risky and I find it hard to continue with the task.

21. I always think things will turn out badly or that I will fail and that stops me from going on.

22. I prefer to accomplish smaller things that give me pleasure than to work on important goals that would improve my life but take time to achieve.

23. I become upset when I have to postpone things that give me pleasure.

24. Even if something isn't that important, if it is bothering me, I can't ignore it and it distracts me from other, more important things.

25. I often find it hard to stay on track.

26. I think of things that are not related to what I am supposed to be working on, and I suspend the task at hand to do something different.

27. I know I am going to get into trouble by putting off an important task, but I do it anyway.

28. I put off doing things I don't feel like doing.
29. I wait until the last minute to do even the most important things.

30. I find it hard to do much more than start new projects or tasks, and once I get them started, I suspend them without completing them.

31. I think I should stop procrastinating but I repeat my mistakes without changing my behavior.

32. I try to focus on the task at hand but I get distracted before I know it.

33. I waste a lot of time. (Yes, this is being asked again, this is common in actual scientific testing.)

34. Your other personal challenge goes here....

OK, let's see what results you've discovered in a general form:

If you answered 'yes' or 'sometimes' to 1-10 of these questions, you are probably pretty average. Sometimes, you feel overwhelmed and find it hard to focus or start new tasks, even if they are important. But, most of the time you avoid procrastination. You're attaining your goals and desired outcomes in life as long as you are indeed setting those goals and desired outcomes!
  If you answered 'yes or 'sometimes' to 11-20 of these questions, you have a challenge, and you should look at the areas in your life where you most often procrastinate, or the types of things you tend to put off. Get to the root of the problem

and use the ideas I gave you last week to eliminate procrastination.

If you answered 'yes' or 'sometimes' to 21-34 of these questions, you are a person who really cares about yourself! You took the time to take a hard look at yourself and honestly see what is up in your life. You spend a lot of your time trying to catch up, doing things at the last minute - and not very well - and explaining your way out of jams. You should seriously consider the things you find difficult to do and determine what is holding you back. Use this information to establish a personal plan to prevent procrastination.

It's easy to say that self-sabotage is at the root of most procrastination. It may be at the root of all procrastination.

And what is self-sabotage? Self-sabotage is an act that, if you did it to someone else, it would be cruel or even criminal. Doing it to yourself makes your life nearly impossible to manage. Begin to notice when you do things that "feel" tiring or overwhelming, but are actually in your best long term interest.

Kevin Hogan

Chapter Six

How Your Current Goals System Completely Failed You

I t's frustrating. You've identified the roots of your procrastination, the delay factor. Time Management should now be a snap. But the planning systems still won't work because they are all based on flawed Goal Setting Pseudo-Science.

Don't get me wrong, some of the parts of the equation are obvious and almost everyone has them right, but the number of problems easily outweighs the number of factors that are in order. Similarly there is YOU!

You are well intended. You are smart. You are not a loser. You are stressed to the max. Everything new you wanted to accomplish in the first part of this year has either failed, or you haven't put in motion. You aren't alone. One of the biggest pieces of the systematic Time Management failure comes from Competing Commitments.

Competing Commitments and The Power of Weakness

Let's go back inside, but this time, let's avoid the more abstract metaphor and get to the concrete metaphors and the raw science.

There is the part I call, YOU, your conscious mind: explicit, logical, emotional, rational; and there is also the reactive part of you, the much more powerful "implicit mind." The implicit mind is the non-conscious, non-thinking, highly reactive part of your mind...the part that actually drives your car while you (consciously) talk to the person sitting in the other seat.

The reactive part of your mind is that part which is, in large part, pre-programmed to do things well that you already do over and over again....and it comes installed for you, totally ready to survive.... and has been for two million years. Or, if you wish, God programmed you that way at creation. Either way, the result is the same. Your genes are plugged in to survival.

Your genes don't (directly) tell you to store nuts like a squirrel. **Your genes don't CAUSE you to DO much of anything**

81

except survive, have sex (reproduce), find food and flee from danger or eliminate the danger.

From these four factors come 16 core desires that shape your behavior within every context...and every context shapes your behavior. And, of course, part of that "implicit mind" was also shaped, particularly when you were young. There are very few contexts or environments that exist that encourage longevity, happiness, success, achievement, long-term security, or anything else that benefits your family and those you love...or yourself.

The 16 Core Desires are discussed in *Covert Hypnosis: An Operator's Manual*. Here they are merely listed to give you a hint of what is driving your brain.

1) Desire to Flee from or Fight Danger/Tranquility
2) Desire for Sex or to Reproduce
3) Desire to Eat
4) Desire for Vengeance or to Compete
5) Drive to Nest
6) Drive to Connect with Others
7) Drive for Power
8) Drive for Status
9) Desire for Independence
10) Drive of Curiosity
11) Desire for Acceptance
12) Desire of Principled Loyalty
13) Drive of Altruism
14) Desire for Order
15) Drive to Save
16) Desire for Physical Activity

The inner drives were first catalogued by William James and since his original work, the most current and up to date collection is what we use here as originally tabulated by Stephen Reiss.

The Power of The Core Instinctual Drives

I want you to THINK about HOW you FEEL when you are eating food you lust after, like chocolate. I want you to THINK about how you FEEL when you experience the deep pleasure of sex. I want you to think about how you feel when you escape or overcome danger. I want you to think about what compares to those things.

No one has ever run this by you, but here is the reality of life...

KEYPOINT: The experiences/feelings that are the fulfillment of those core instinctual drives that media and society call "addictions," provide so much pleasure in the moment that they are unequaled by acting on other drives. The overall PQ (pleasure quotient) of each of the four drivers is unparalleled. Only conscious choice and breaking orbit can "overcome" the downside of the core drives.

So, if you were defeating enemies, having sex and then eating chocolate all day, you probably wouldn't want cocaine or an opiate to relax with later. These "secondary addictions" are all strong "fulfillments" of the core drives and desires, as well. Unfortunately when food, sex, avoidance of discomfort and the easy life are abundant, it becomes difficult to break orbit and experience everything else in life.

Why are your goals and management of your life and time, in jeopardy of never being accomplished? It's pretty simple, really. Here is what you tried to do, discovered, and then failed at, and why "it all" couldn't work even if you had wanted it to.

Goals are Not "Comfort"-able

You set a "goal" and then moments or days or weeks later, you have the opportunity to sleep, rest, meditate, bliss out, putter, play, you name it...it makes no difference...ANYTHING is better in the moment than WORKING TOWARD a goal.

By its nature, a goal is typically something that is NOT in the status quo. **Goals are not comfortable. They induce stress and require change.** Ants and squirrels spend their lives building a life and giving them survival advantages in harsh environments. The vast majority of people (to be referred to from here on as "people") don't do so beyond bare minimums. They aren't comfortable with the unfamiliar and they aren't familiar with discomfort....and ANYTHING feels better than being outside of a comfort zone.

One of the most important factors of a scientific time management system is the very simple act of having triggers or lists on a table or desk that you will see and be reminded of all day.

Put your system on a computer and your life is not going to change. Scout's Honor.

And goal setting and getting....oh my...the end result of what will be a great time management system you and I are creating is so simple to say, and so difficult to achieve. You and I simply want to achieve our goals and dreams. That's it.

Fighting with the wife...much easier than moving toward a goal. Going to the horrifying office...much easier than moving toward a goal. Being an ongoing victim of violence...much easier than moving toward a goal.

For people, just about anything is more comfortable and feels more familiar than moving toward a goal, and people will do that which feels comfortable and familiar. People will fight with the wife, get beat up by the spouse, be an ongoing victim of violence, because it is familiar and comfortable to the brain so long as ultimate survival is not threatened and...survival appears to be enhanced.

KEYPOINT: The vast majority of humankind does only what is absolutely necessary for raw survival.

People Don't Change and Everybody Lies

The cynical Dr. House (M.D.), the character on the TV show, says that, "People don't change." "Everybody lies." I have a t-shirt that says "Everybody Lies," and that, of course, refers to everyone, except you and me. Now, many would say that those are cynical points of view. Let's look at that for a minute.

True or False? People don't change.

Fact: People don't change and barely even "shift" or "move."

People marry a girl from down the street or someone with the same last initial (or the next letter in the alphabet) because she sat next to the guy in school or had the locker next to him. We don't move much, for anything.

Lazy feels comfortable. It feels familiar and it feels like tranquility, the opposite of flight/fight. That is why Achievers are remarkably different. Achievers intentionally shape themselves or have been shaped by their environment to be a group that thrives on change. *Only Achievers who want to control their own destiny, set goals AND use the will and power to overcome their inherent desire for comfort, their weaknesses and personal flaws to do anything meaningful in life.* Perhaps 10% of people are "fortunate" enough to choose to change...to thrive on change...to need change. And of course "fortune" had nothing to do with not being a "normal person."

True or False? Everybody lies.

Fact: Yes, everybody lies. Deception is absolutely necessary for survival, and, typically, for reproduction and definitely for flight and fight. People are pretty good at deception, though 20% or so excel at it. Some for good, some for evil.

So, for the most part, Dr. House (MD) is correct. People don't change. You can predict people's behavior much easier than you can the weather. If the guy had terrible sales numbers last quarter, he'll almost certainly have terrible numbers this quarter. People will do tomorrow what they did today. Major corporations spend BILLIONS on market research on what products and services will catch on. The research is wrong well in excess of 95% of the time.

Is it Possible for People to Change? Can a Time Management System even Work?

The better question is: Can people who set goals, people who are "normal" people of laziness and perhaps sloth, and definitely from the realm of entitlement ever become... change into...people of achievement and actually MOVE toward their GOALS?

Fact: Yes. But...it takes a few things to make it happen.

Environmental Change happens when you take the person out of their current home or office or classroom and move them to another that is significantly different.

Contextual Change occurs when you change the "why" of something. For example, I didn't do the dishes and you are upset with me. But then I tell you I just got back from taking a friend to the hospital. The context of the situation has changed in your mind.

KEYPOINT: In order for Time Management and Goal Achievement strategies to work, environmental and contextual changes ARE REQUIRED.

The Single Most Important Factor in Change and Achievement?

In other words, the environment, (which is almost always a contextual change) and the context are the MOST important factors in your behavior. *If you don't change your environment and context, you will not change.* Period.

If you don't change the most dynamic influences in your life, you will not change. Those influences are often other people. People will either push you to change. (We call them pushy people) or... People will reinforce normal human behavior, to accept welfare, unemployment, to take from those who achieve and redistribute by threat of force and threat of imprisonment to those who do almost nothing to generate value or growth of culture and the environment.

That is predictable. Here's the cycle on a larger scale then we'll look at it in your life.

The Stages of Societies

Most societies at most stages of their history will be in an "Entitlement" stage about HALF of the life cycle of a culture. There are other stages that lead to entitlement.

There is the "Discovery" or "Movement" stage where people find a new land or place or place to work. Usually because they are FORCED TO MOVE or CHANGE.

There is the "Settlement" stage where the people who just experienced months or years of dramatic change "settle in" and establish occupations to create value for the environment.

There is the "Doctrine of Inequality" stage where the 80% who don't contribute to the value of the environment become angry and decide to punish the 20% who do contribute and redistribute wealth, which never works because the 90% of people who are comfort creatures absorb all wealth only to be entitled to more. Note the overlap, I'll come back to this later.

And then the society dies and is taken over by another society that is in the "Discovery" or "Movement" stage.

People's Lives Mimic the Stages of Societies

The same is true for 80-90% of people's lives on an individual level. Some cultures require goals in the harshest of settings...often a requirement for achieving in the long-term.

In China, the poor save 30 cents per day toward their future. That's about 30% of their income! In America, people save about four percent (per year/decade) toward their future... for incomes that are 150 TIMES greater than the Chinese (on average).

Don't misunderstand, people save perhaps 4% in their retirement funds...it will be gone because of "an emergency" or uncomfortable time in the near future. It's not likely to make it to retirement. I'll show you this in crystal clear glass later in the book.

Why? Necessity. There is no necessity in America to save (up until today) because there is no punishment of laziness in the context of the environment. And, interestingly, in the last decade, our country has talked about one of the last pillars to fall in free societies in the 21st century...national health care. If people don't earn it, people can feel entitled to it and be given it. In China, if people don't save, people will starve. It is that simple. Necessity IS the Mother of Invention....and the Politics of Destruction.

A Mentor Can Help You Achieve Goals

In order to Achieve Goals You Probably NEED a Coach, a Mentor. I can't think of anyone who didn't have a good personal advisor or coach that achieved in life. Here's what the pretend-a-guru will tell you about your goals: "Work a little each day on your goals." Moron. Idiot. Fool. Guaranteed recipe for failure. It's just not real.

The client had already, "done a little each day." In fact they'd probably done a "little" each day for 20 years. People spend nine hours each day busting their butts at "a job" which gets them nothing but the status quo and a life that REQUIRES balance or insanity will kick in. A life where they must return to the hamster wheel next month or they will be on the street. (The individual level of the end of society.)

It's going to require something close to that to CHANGE and ACHIEVE something that MEANS something. "OK Mr. Ant, just go do five minutes each day..." "OK Mr. Squirrel, just go collect nuts for about 10 minutes each day..."

If you get a coach that tells you to do the same things you've been doing for the last 20 years, get a new coach. You don't need to be a billionaire nor do you need to save the world from its impending disasters. You probably would be wise to prepare for an uncertain future because to do otherwise would be counter-wise...by definition: foolish.

So, what DO you do if you can't afford a First Class coach?

Become Significant and live...a life with M
where you are SIGNIFICANT to some group (
at LEAST some person is not only a good
requisite for achieving goals.

If there was anyone watching "up there," I'd want her/him to look down and say, "Damn good job, Kev. You screwed up pretty bad on Z but you got X and Y, good goin'."

Either you are a person of significance or you are not. But remember not to judge others. There is nothing evil or bad about people who don't act on their goals. That IS the predicted result for the vast majority of people. It takes MUCH directed and focused action each day to bend the instincts of the non-conscious drivers in people's lives. For most people, they **simply will do anything to avoid the departure from tranquility or familiarity.** *People consider it ridiculous to be uncomfortable...they do everything they can to be the opposite. And that is natural, normal and to be expected.*

The question, of course, is: Will you be "people" or will YOU achieve what YOU set out to DO, to change, to live better not only for yourself but for those you love and for those you wish to create significance for?

Warning: Parts of this section might be particularly painful to read and very politically incorrect...only problem....it is all ...the facts...

Not too long ago, you were all fired up and eager to move ahead on your New Year Resolutions or whatever you called them. You set your "Sixty Days to Success in 20XX" or "Ninety Days to Gnarly Results" or something equally as cute or maybe, "2010 my life will be Zen." The year of your breakthrough? Result... Nothing. Oh, wait there is a result.... How do you feel about yourself upon brief analysis?

Like garbage. Embarrassed for yourself, though maybe not to others...yet. You've even tried to place or project the blame and responsibility from yourself to someone else. You'd have been better off not setting goals because, frankly, this is the result you get most of the time.

You put a LOT of thought into your goals, got clear about the changes you wanted to make, you conceived a genius plan that would undoubtedly change your life forever, and waited for that magical date... January 1st to arrive.... After all, the holidays are no time to set goals...goals conflict with family and family comes first. (If you had that set of thoughts, you had guaranteed failure from square one.)

When the clock struck midnight on December 31st, it was full steam ahead! You were off to a great start and confidently began taking the steps you knew would lead you directly to the life of your dreams!

And then . . . maybe a couple of days later, maybe even a couple of weeks later, you began losing steam. At first it may have been small things, like bumping into a few minor obstacles or struggling to find time to work on your goals consistently; but before you knew it, you found yourself feeling unmotivated, tired, angry, frustrated . . . and finally wondered what you were thinking when you set these stupid goals, anyway. You must have been out of your mind to think that you could achieve something so big - you've never been able to do it before, right? And no one supported you in the first place when you told them....and instead of going out and proving them wrong, your non-conscious mind "figured out" the simplest way for you to go on living with the least amount of effort possible.

STOP HERE. Two things before we go on.

1. **Your non-conscious doesn't "figure out" anything. It is like a computer preloaded with software. It either does or doesn't do stuff based on what is already on the computer.** If you have a neat photo album program but it doesn't allow for photo editing and extensive touch ups, then you would have to buy a program like Photoshop, download, learn it, and then you would use it. Because that doesn't happen in your real life very often, your non-conscious requires very little

"maintenance." It just keeps on ticking as it is. the bus that is your brain.

2. Second, "your goals." Don't "have goals" that you are going to "work on." You don't "work on" goals. You work on the engine of a car or you go cut your lawn. **You achieve goals...or not.**

What is a goal SUPPOSED to be, anyway?

A goal is really what you want your life to be like or something you want in your life every day beginning (ideally) at some period of time. You don't work on "achieving goals," instead you want to "work on" designing, say, July 17, in a specific location, office, with a certain person, with different lifestyle habits, and so forth.

TODAY (when you have a goal) just like at the end of the day today, you will have done certain things and not done others. If you didn't exercise today, you didn't want to; you chose not to. It's that simple. If you want to assure yourself that you will exercise July 17, you need to have it be habitual long before you arrive at that date.

Between your conscious and non-conscious mind, **unless you have truly decided to take control of your life, your non-conscious will invariably win all "choice wars."**

KEYPOINT: Your "Conscious choices" will require you to have new *non-preloaded* software that you must: buy, learn to use, download, test, use daily, and become proficient.

Ugh. Much easier to just stick with what you have.

Oh, don't get me wrong. You got "busy for awhile." You did "action steps" and even went to the gym, started a diet, all kinds of things that seemingly made it obvious that you were on your way to a "new life."

91

Whether the above scenario describes your situation exactly or not, it stands as a common example of how easy it is to set goals, especially "seasonally-planned goals" like New Year's Resolutions... and how difficult it can be to follow through and actually achieve them. Most people whom I know that fail do the following really.... STUPID (sorry, but it's true) things.

5 Stupid Things People Do That Lead to Failure

1) They set a 1-3 year goal that was so stupidly outrageous that they couldn't wrap their mind around it.

Example: This year they earned $50,000 and they set a goal for next year for $1,000,000. Dumb, dumb, dumb, dumb...dumb, doobey doobey...dumb.....might as well "set a goal for winning the lottery."
Your non-conscious laughs.
Think of ALL of your friends you talked to who believed in *"The Secret"*. I'm not talking about the millionaires who promote and sell *"The Secret"*, I'm talking about the normal human beings like you who earned less than $75,000 annually as of say, two years ago. Those people.
Did you notice them all become wealthy, happy and healthy because they believed in *"The Secret"*?
Exactly. Nothing changed.
Not with any of them. None. No one. Because they didn't do ANYTHING we talked about that is necessary for changes to happen. They rubbed their Magic Lamp and the Genie came out and said, "What are you, Stupid?"

2) Your friends set all kinds of short-term goals that were achievable that really meant nothing. (Put up a web site, call one hour of cold calling per day, go to gym daily. Eat healthy. Spend Saturday with kids and two hours per day with wife.)

If putting up a web site is a goal, you are 100% screwed. Putting up a web site is what you do before you go to bed tonight, not make it a "goal" for next week. Bluntly...do you set a goal to go the bathroom? That's the equivalent of putting up a web site.

You HAVE to go to the bathroom and you MUST have a web site up.

3) You *only* set a 20-year or life set of goals, and that…. is ridiculous.

Reality check: You have NO clue what life will be like 20 years from now and can't fathom what will be going on in life, so this ranks as one of the most ridiculous activities you can waste your time on.

4) You spend a half hour with your goals each day as if they were people.

You NEED to spend about 1 minute with your mid-term goals each day and then about three minutes on the core stuff that needs to get done THAT DAY and then go about doing them, until they are done.

5) You spend hours writing down your values and beliefs.

You do this instead of spending two hours writing down what YOU WANT your values and beliefs to be INSTEAD of what HAS BEEN important to you up until now that has caused 100% abject failure.

Yep, a total 100% waste of time. Be comforted by one thing. Here we are 40 or 140 or 240 days into 20XX and I promise you only 1/1000 people who were not used to "getting things done" are doing much of anything toward... anything.

- Maybe the wife wasn't supportive (who cares).
- Maybe the kids didn't realize this was as much for them as anyone. (Too bad)
- Maybe you just couldn't get past flat out laziness to bust butt an extra 4-10 hours per day and instead set "just an hour a day to success" goals that could never have worked in the first place.

So what's going on? You know all of this. You rebalanced your life like tires on a car, right to where it is now 100% out of balance and right on a disaster path into the teeth of the tornado. Now those are the big reasons most people fail. But there are others. WAIT!

Even if it's not the beginning of the year, you can STILL have July 17 (or October 25, or December 1...) be part of your new life, if you demand that your conscious mind take control over your non-conscious mind. You can STILL have what you want in life. You can STILL be relevant in the world and help the people who need help in the world. or...you can do the same thing you keep doing year after year, which is - giving in to the natural patterns of your life.

You've been awakened. You've been given second life. You don't have to use the goal setting you've been using; but definitely don't use the goal setting ideas THEY taught you.

Because....they will fail, too....Here's why...

Watching how the tragedy of Hurricane Katrina in Louisiana and Mississippi play out taught us more than just the fact that government doesn't belong in charge of anything important. Katrina and its aftermath taught us all a great deal about human nature. I want to utilize powerful examples of what happened in the deep South, along with some fallacies of "self-help" texts in order to reveal what does, and does not work in goal setting. Best of all, the stuff that does work has been validated to be scientifically correct. In other words, we know it works and it's been proven.

But first.... Imagine...

You finally have a Noillim! You lucked out? You worked hard? Whatever, now you have a Noillim!!! Congratulations. You did affirmations? "I want a Noillim. I want a Noillim. I want a Noillim!!!!"

Doesn't do much, does it? Doesn't take someone with an MBA to figure out that generally speaking, you don't get what you can't see. You don't know what a Noillim even looks like? You don't know what it is? You can't imagine owning a Noillim. And that's the first reason goal setting as you were taught simply doesn't work. It can't for three reasons.

The Key to Goal Setting That Works

You can't have a Noillim until you know what it is, what it looks like, how to utilize it, what it can do for you, the challenges you will have when you have it, the work you will have to do to acquire it, the steps it will require, the time that should be reasonably expected.

A Noillim is something everyone says they wish they had. But only 1/100 will ever have that much. Oh wait! Yeah, yeah. I'm pretty clever when it comes to codes... Noillim....Backwards that spells...Million! A million dollars. Sorry about that! I had it backwards. How silly can I be?

That's the first reason the goal setting system you were taught will fail. If a person can't get "inside" of a million dollars and see just what that is, what that provides, how to experience it...it simply won't manifest. The affirmations and positive attitude simply won't work. They can't. But then, there is more. For many years they told you that if you just can imagine your goal, in rich detail, in every respect, everything about it, you can have it. Doesn't work.

I had a richly painted picture of a safe, clean, habitable and back to normal New Orleans in my mind today... along with thousands of other good-hearted people. Result? You guessed it. BUT...Here is a FACT: If you can develop enough pain to be associated to the present mess, you can probably jump out of the mess. BUT...Here is another FACT: People still won't do it because they don't understand where they are going.

Doesn't work.

What does? Does ANYTHING work in goal setting? Is it all just a bunch of hogwash??

The Science of Split Screen Thinking

The research is showing that successful goal setting requires a richly and easily imagined target AND a stark contrast to the present...almost contemporaneously. In other words, you think of the goal, and then you think present. Then you think goal. You set the two side by side. This creates cognitive dissonance. (You get annoyed and must solve!) That's where your brain begins to go to work on constructing a bridge from here to there.

> **KEYPOINT: The achievement factor is born in the contrast between the status quo moving into the future and standing it next to your preferred and desired life.**

When two diverse realities exist, the person is compelled to solve and make one real. Given two sets of information very different from each other, you feel compelled to get from point to point and make ONE picture. One reality. One experience. Two is not how the brain is comfortable and content.

But even split screen thinking, which gives birth to dissatisfaction and dissonance, is only SQUARE ONE. Picturing "a better life" (if you will) and contrasting it with today, creates the dissatisfaction, but there is still inertia. Nothing has happened to lead me to believe that this "better life" can be MY reality. Just because I see it means nothing. Seeing it contrasted to the present is a very good thing indeed. But you and I need to be CONVINCED that it is attainable and that **the fear of failing to achieve it is not greater than overcoming the inertia to begin moving toward it.**

Why Don't People Change and/or "Do What's Right"?

What is it that causes people to stop moving toward the split screen picture that has been shown to be effective?

The present environment is so utterly normal and familiar that it is very hard for the brain to adapt to new realities no matter how appealing and how good they make you feel.

I took family and friends for a trip to Las Vegas. We stayed at The Mirage. Penthouse Suite. Best service money can buy. Everything. But it was our first time there. On our third night in town, we decided to see KA, a Cirque de Soleil show at the MGM Grand, which is where we typically stay when we go with the six of us. As we walked into the front door of one of the world's largest hotels, two of the girls spontaneously said, "Now I feel like I'm home." And frankly, so did I.

Where Will Your Brain Naturally Guide You?

To leave that which is utterly familiar is EXTREMELY DIFFICULT for the human brain to make happen.

The inertia is everything at the emotional and instinctual level of reaction.

KEYPOINT: The brain will guide you to the MOST FAMILIAR actions and results.

In New Orleans, residents had to be COAXED to leave their destroyed homes a week AFTER the storm had hit, destroyed everything, started the process of disease and though people knew it "made sense" to leave, many just "couldn't."

Of course! To leave that which is familiar and go to the unfamiliar is very, very, very hard to get the brain to do and you DO have to get the brain to DO IT, because it will not guide you to the most logical actions.

Only through great will can someone break free of the familiar.

The good news, is, that you have that will, within you! It's just rarely activated, as you already know.

Living YOUR LIFE is now easier because there is finally a process that works. Ready?!

Kevin Hogan

Chapter Seven

The Ultimate Key to Success in Your Lifetime

C ould a chapter in a book really be worth $100,000? Seems like a pretty tall order and pretty puffy claim.

And this chapter contains the first-ever $100,000 Key I've laid out in any book I've written. Perhaps 15 times per year, I put a $10,000 key in an article I write for my e-zine, *Coffee with Kevin Hogan*. These golden nuggets have value that if used, well, they are better than gold. If not, they are absolutely worthless. The single most profound piece of information for achievement and success that I've ever written about is in this Chapter. Pass it along to your friends.

I know your intention is pure. You truly want to do something to make your life mean something. You get part of the richness of life through your relationships. You get another part of the zest for living through your lifestyle and how you spend your time. You get another part of your life meaning from your work. Maybe...You pick something that sounds fun, interesting, challenging or something that has a support system...like franchising or network marketing...can be a dandy Coffee Table business.

Another possibility? Internet affiliate programs are some of the easiest, fastest ways to build wealth. They might be one or two-tiered, either is fine and they DO qualify as a true entrepreneurial venture. That means YOU determine whether you will succeed or not. It's hard to say a person has 100% control in anything in life, but on the Internet you have about as much control and self-determinism as you can get in life.

Of course, there are hundreds and thousands of entrepreneurial avenues you could choose to play in, in addition to your 8-5 work. I decided to name two CONCRETE examples because otherwise you wouldn't move in that direction...for your first solo venture, you'll probably pick a business that doesn't require recruiting.

You might do any of a lot of things, but you finally DO something. You start the "going into the micro business process." The thinking process goes OK. The planning process goes OK.

The first phone calls or Internet interactions are new and definitely uncomfortable. Uh oh.... Because selling or marketing is uncomfortable, or making your first website is uncomfortable or whatever, you decide in short order that this is probably "wrong for you."

I was talking with a friend who was getting ready to start a service business earlier this week. A recession buster he thought. The business? Duct cleaning. Everyone needs clean ducts...

"My marketing plan is to hang those things from door knobs. I'll service the people who call in."

"You'll go broke."

That hurts so bad to say that. It hurts worse to hear it. The person thinks you're (me) "being negative."

Not at all.

I'm just saving them $100,000, bankruptcy and their future. It takes almost no time to borrow $100,000, start a business and kill it, and then wonder why it happened, or what went wrong.

KEYPOINT: Where things go wrong is at the intersection of you and your discomfort.

When you do something you aren't familiar with, or comfortable with, or you inherently don't like, you rarely will find the stick-to-it-iveness to continue.

Let's break this down to what happened to you...

Whatever it was, you got this FEELING inside that you couldn't make the phone call or knock on the door or make the website. (Any of these actions requires no mental skill whatsoever. Children aged 6 can successfully do any or all of these things.) Or, you couldn't get past writing the third chapter. Or you got the web page up but trying to figure out the program for the page was too frustrating. The page eventually got up....but...YOU got down. You FELT badly. You felt a bit depressed. You felt like you KNEW you were doing the wrong business model. You might have gotten angry. You might have cursed. "IT" DIDN'T WORK. And this, of course, is the likely result. People truly think that "it" doesn't "work." Or the better and more definitive cop out...."It wasn't meant to be."

Here's the hard truth. Write this down on paper, paint it on the wall. Post it on your computer.

- It has nothing to do with a positive attitude.
- It has nothing to do with what you "believe."
- It has nothing to do with positive thinking.
- It has nothing to do with working smarter instead of harder.
- It has nothing to do with having your intentions aligned with the universe and attracting something.
- It has nothing to do with what was meant to be.
- It has nothing to do with "The Secret".

So just what Platinum Nugget could possibly be worth $100,000 and create more time for love and stress release? Consider this:

When you regularly "fail" at something that a child can do, you didn't do two things that are necessary for success:

1. You didn't CONTINUE until it was DONE.
2. You didn't walk through the fire of discomfort, pain and fear.

- ❖ You quit when it got hard.
- ❖ You quit when it got frustrating.
- ❖ You got tired.
- ❖ You got angry.
- ❖ You were upset.
- ❖ You were apathetic.

You let your feelings get in the way of what you wanted in life and then to make it all OK, you posited:

a) It doesn't work or,
b) Who really wants to do X, anyway?

101

There are a lot of people being suckered right now by a popular book that tells you to get in alignment with your feelings for things to work out. If you do that...it is a 100% guarantee that you will ultimately fail. Don't misunderstand...Feelings aren't the "enemy." There's not a thing wrong with feeling upset, angry, tired, apathetic, happy or sad. Feelings are a wake-up call that you have not become comfortable in a specific life experience.

Feelings of discomfort "talk to you." **They say to you that you belong in your hamster wheel**...but you misinterpret them to read, "This other thing I've been dreaming about isn't right for me. It's certainly not necessary."

Feelings aren't very smart. They have zero IQ. Interpreting something with no "sense" to it is something no one is taught in school or anywhere else. And it's not your fault.

No one ever taught you how to TRULY understand feelings. Without going into a big long diatribe on neuro-psychology, feelings and emotions, let's just put it this way: You simply can't live your life based on your feelings in the moment or you will be doing all the things that "feel good" all the time...addiction. And like the mice in experiments where they are given endless quantities of any addictive substance, they do not move. They sit, psychologically paralyzed and starve to death...and it felt good.

Drive your life on your feelings and you fail as a parent, a spouse, a lover, a neighbor, a leader in your church, in business. You miss out on everything that matters.

And, you fail fast.

"Honey would you feed the baby?"

"I haven't slept in a week. I'm too exhausted. Would you please?"

"No can do. I don't feel like it. My feelings aren't aligned with my intention to watch the game."

Baby dies. Oh well. At least they felt good. People who run their lives based on their feelings become addicts of "feeling good and avoid feeling anything painful or bad."

It's only human nature. And the addict won't change. Feeling "good" is simply too fun and easy...until they take the furniture, the house and the kids. **When you walk through the fire of your feelings, fear and pain, you WILL ULTIMATELY** come to the point that your new actions become familiar. This is what no one teaches. It can take a week or two or three or four depending on how much you are involved. It doesn't take long but getting past the first day or two or three is a toughie.

$100,000 KEYPOINT ACTION: Walk through the fire of your feelings, experience the fear and live through the pain, however brief, and you will ultimately FEEL COMFORTABLE and FAMILIAR with all of the NEW ASPECTS of Life/Experience/Business/Relationship.

That is the key to success in life, love, wealth and meaning. Should have been more complicated than that. That's worth writing down and taping on your computer...in your planner....writing on the top of each day of your journal...right? Because, once you do THIS ONE THING...you conquer almost every challenge in life. Then all you really need is momentum.

MOMENTUM

Remember those old pieces of footage from when NASA would launch an Apollo rocket to the moon? That big Saturn rocket that carried the teeny tiny lunar module on top...the one with Neil Armstrong, Buzz Aldrin, Jim Collins....that Saturn V rocket was over 350 FEET tall. I've stood next to the lunar module that came back from the moon, and it's about 10 feet high and it's hard to believe you could squish a few people in that little thing.

Back to the Saturn V, though.

I am *not* a rocket scientist but these missions fascinated me. Those huge rockets were actually built in three different parts (stages). The first stage was the big one. It was the base. It was what gave the initial burst of oomph to get the rocket and it's passengers in the air.

That first stage was 138' tall. It burned 4.4 MILLION POUNDS of fuel in just 150 SECONDS. That took the rocket a grand total of 42 miles on its 250,000-mile trip to the moon. **42/250,000…the first 42 miles and it used 80% of the fuel for a HALF MILLION mile trip!**

Then the stage was ejected and it fell back to earth somewhere in an ocean. The rocket was now flying at over 6,000 miles per hour. Then stage two kicked in. **Stage two was 81' tall** and used 1 MILLION POUNDS of fuel in just 6 minutes and pushed the rocket **another 109 miles** to a speed of 15,000 miles+ per hour.

So you have this 350+ foot rocket and in **the first 9 MINUTES 96% of all the FUEL used** to gain momentum was used for the first 109/250,000 of the mission TO the moon AND BACK. (Remember the passengers had to get back home, too!)

Stage three was 58 feet tall and this stage was a little more complex and I frankly don't get how it all worked but basically it pushed the remainder of the rocket for about 6 MINUTES (as little as 2.5 minutes and as much as almost three hours) to get the rocket really rocking around the earth so it could "slingshot" out of earth's atmosphere and off to the moon, then it would bring the passengers into orbit around the moon. (All of the science is beyond my comprehension.) **This final stage used 250,000 pounds of fuel, or about 4% of the total FUEL for 99.9% of the remainder of the trip of there and back!** That boggles my mind to this day.

When I was a little kid my grandparents lived in Huntsville, Alabama and my brothers and myself would visit them in the summer time. One of the "stages" of the rocket(s) was kept in Huntsville at a NASA facility. We got a chance to see it and it triggered even further fascination into the idea of MOMENTUM.

EVERYTHING HAPPENS in the first few SECONDS or MINUTES. If you break earth's gravitational pull, inertia, then you can accomplish anything. You have to get started, and CONTINUE. It's hard at first then you break gravitational pull and the orbit of the STATUS QUO and you are OFF and the rest becomes almost easy.

Momentum is SO important. **If you dedicate 10 hours per day, 7 days per week, to your project X *for six weeks*, it will**

be almost a sure thing that you will succeed over the next 10 YEARS with Project X.

Your life will COMPLETELY change. You will be COMPLETELY transformed. You will be CAPABLE of just about anything that is humanly possible. But only a teeny tiny percentage of people will be willing to be that uncomfortable for say, six weeks.

Because most people can't get past discomfort for any period longer than moments, few people accomplish...anything. There is no meaning to be had because there is no discomfort; there is no sense of unfamiliarity.

Meaning comes when something is not comfortable.

You can use 95% of the energy on a project and fail, exhausted with the remaining third stage falling back to earth...or you can use the 96th% and break free from gravity...which is really just getting past inertia and started and then it's not unfamiliar or uncomfortable anymore. Then it's simply a wise use of time.

The great life lesson, perhaps the greatest and most important lesson is knowing this in advance: **The danger is that you WILL feel un-rewarded for the energy you expend on a project with no return.** People are used to getting a paycheck every two weeks and no table top business will return a dollar in the first two weeks but you'll be working two or three times as hard at the Coffee Table business as you are at work.

Your family will be upset with you because you are grumpy. You will be tired and have nothing to show for your work.

The TEMPTATION to QUIT is OVERWHELMING ESPECIALLY IF YOU ARE DOING WHAT WORKS..., which is why it takes 5.5 MILLION POUNDS OF FUEL to go 109/250,000 miles and only 0.2 MILLION POUNDS OF FUEL to go 499,881 miles. (Remember you have to get back!)

No one knows that...except you.

Obviously this could be a relationship, a business, anything. All of the hardest work on your part is early on when everything is unfamiliar and uncomfortable. All of the smart work is the rest of the project. So isn't it worth planning your day, your life so that you are constantly REMINDING YOURSELF DAILY to

CONTINUE if you are in the first 109 miles AND challenging yourself to do things that you would be proud of yourself for?

That is one of the fatal flaws of almost all (perhaps all) time planning systems in existence. Nothing is more important than the advance reminder that the unfamiliar and uncomfortable is anticipated and prepared for.

But no matter how much preparation or planning you do, it WILL BE UNCOMFORTABLE & UNFAMILIAR. You will feel like you want to jump back into your comfort zone. Period.

Remember, you already work 8 hours a day plus commuting. Then you have family stress, neighbor stress, sick kids, funerals and weddings, phone calls, emails...and you now are aware that you will be in your own personally designed Life Boot Camp when you initiate new projects. It's the nature of life. It's the nature of MEANING. It's the nature of success.

But that is not the nature of the NATURAL DESIRED STATE of a human. Humans want BALANCE when they get home. The pull for BALANCE is OVERWHELMING...just like the rocket launch. **Meaning, however, enters life when there is significant discomfort and unfamiliarity present.**

Women will go through discomfort for 9 MONTHS to just to "make a baby." (Men, if you think you were that important, even if you went to the baby classes, you're so self-deluded that you'll never make it in business. You went to the classes for one reason. To convince your wife you were worth not killing.) Women go 9 months...but men? The guy won't spend 9 WEEKS to create a permanent stable financial support system for the baby and Mom. (And you wonder why we are expendable as men?)

Realize that Mom is pregnant 24/7. There is no "longer day." They are all long. And I'm flat out serious. Oh, and don't think I'm being politically correct. Two years later Mom will go to a job and get paid less than a man because she missed two years of whirlwind changes in business that she couldn't humanly have kept up with.

Success and Meaning in Life is about reality. People who whine that something is too hard: I got no problem with that. People who whine that something is too hard and don't DO ANYTHING TO OVERCOME IT, I got a big problem with that.

What's a real shame is that people TRULY BELIEV
building their own small Coffee Table business, w......
something they have chosen, something they personally find
interesting, something that might actually be rewarding, *is
harder* than running the hamster wheel every day for the rest of
their life (until they retire). And they are right...for the first six
weeks before breaking earth's atmosphere...but only the few ever
will break free.

Just think about THAT logic! The only thing that is 'harder' is
the work that will be done in the first couple of months while
building momentum. After that nothing compares to the freedom
your own love and interests bring. And you know that every hour
you work, is for you and those who depend on you. But it's darn
tough to get someone to make decisions based upon how they
MIGHT FEEL in two months.

**The PERCEIVED VALUE of some FEELING, or, some
DOLLAR FIGURE in two months is NOTHING compared
to the pain or fear or ANYTHING that you FEEL NOW, in
this moment...**

People run in the moment and only the moment. And that is
why they fail. Without getting all political (this used to be a
better metaphor than it is now), when the woman gets pregnant,
there is no turning back. She toughs it out for nine months and
has a baby. Then toughs it out for 18 years and creates an adult.
Unlike the male, she is fully aware of this because it's all she
thinks about all day long. But men?

Shoot, we don't HAVE TO HAVE a small Coffee Table
business. We don't HAVE to be successful. We don't HAVE to
achieve. We can MAKE IT on what we have going on now in
the hamster wheel as long as nothing horrible happens like
disability or the kids get hurt or they get really sick or go deaf or
blind or yeah...all the things that you can count on ONE
happening but you don't know WHICH one....which is WHY
you MUST set out to achieve NOW.

I want to feel good right now. You want to feel good NOW.
We want the burger, the cigarette, *the whatever feels good in the
moment thing* RIGHT NOW, and the idea of delaying
gratification is simply unheard of. So, we throw out Project X
and go back to being depressed because we are in the hamster

wheel and that is predictable, comfortable and familiar. **The Hamster Wheel is hated but it isn't feared.** It makes no rational sense at all. It's all based on feelings and emotion. It's simply how people act. Very predictable. Very understandable. I commend you for knowing this all in advance. I commend you for talking to all of the people involved in your life about the Saturn V rocket taking off which you can show them on Youtube, for effect.

All of that said, **never** believe that just because something is extremely difficult for six weeks that you will achieve orbit. The difficult part happens when you are doing a lot of unfamiliar and uncomfortable work all day long for those six weeks. If the person has engaged in the work without a plan and a system to get paid for the plan, it almost doesn't matter how hard you work. You didn't add smart to the formula and you can end up never getting close to earth's orbit in the first place.

A good plan is, I'm going to the store. The very first time you need to figure out that entails having a grocery list, getting money, keys to the car, get in the car, open the garage door, exit the garage, don't kill children as you pull out. Take the first right, go one mile, park away from all the other cars, go in and get the stuff on your list. Pay for it all. Bag it all up. Back to car, return trip home, and then put the groceries away.

After that you'll have experienced the discomfort of keeping all that in mind and making sure you did everything. It will seem a lot harder than it really is at the time! The process and results are predictable every single time. Pretty soon it is not uncomfortable and it becomes like cutting the lawn or any other non-thinking process.

Remember the *real* secret:

See, Believe, Begin, Continue, Finish

Those five words summarize it all. The formula. The Golden Key. The real Master Key. Most people can get past the first three and then, of course, they stop. Most people are great starters but don't finish stuff.

"Idea people," is how they refer to themselves. "Idea people" have no self-discipline but will work comfortably (if not irritably) in just about any hamster wheel on the planet. "Idea people" have no tangible value to offer because they can't complete a project. And it's a shame, because it isn't their fault. No one ever taught them CONTINUE AND FINISH.

This is another missing piece of the Time/Life Management puzzle. The "spend just a little time each day," stuff has SOME marginal value, but the fact is it is not much. Continuing and Finishing requires MOMENTUM. They work just as hard as a "finisher" but they don't ever FINISH their IDEA. Thus they have 25 projects that have come to nothing. Successful people aren't worth dollars per hour, they are worth dollars per successfully completed and implemented and managed project.

Each time I sign a new book contract, the publisher doesn't care whether it takes me 2 minutes, 2 hours or 2 years to write the book. I get paid the same no matter what; let's say that's 10%. The publisher doesn't really care if the book is all that "good." That's my reputation on the line. What do they care about? Sales. Period. Is the book going to sell? That's the deal. A publisher doesn't pay minimum wage. They are happy, no, thrilled to pay you $100,000 for your royalties. It's essentially one of the few logical businesses.

You sell 100,000 books, you make $100,000. You sell 1 book, you make $1. Now you know how much you are worth to your publisher. Entitlement schemes that include "benefit packages", minimum wage, stock options are all tossed out the window. There is no "affirmative action". Black people don't get paid more than Indians. Indians don't get paid more than White people. How many books sold?

When you THINK like a writer, you can be successful. It's pretty much the same as thinking like a good farmer.

A writer has to do several things right.
1) Write a book he is proud of. (Makes it easier to write the next book.)
2) Write a book that will sell.
3) Write a book that will sell the writer as worth doing future business with.
4) Sell the book.

5) Get paid.

No stock options. No minimum wage. No guaranteed salary. No raises. No getting fired. No pay reduction. It comes down to ONE thing. PERFORMANCE. You can never whine about your pay as an author (outside of contractual "misunderstandings").

It's the same thing in the music business. Similar, but not quite identical in the movie business. You get paid if people buy your product or service. Period. Think about it. If you want to succeed, to achieve, is there any other way to get paid? If you want to achieve, there never will be another way! Walk through the fire, build momentum and cause this to be central to your Time Plan System.

Time Planning for Meaning is Life Planning for Meaning

The reason it's called a Time Plan System should now be obvious. You aren't letting life happen to you, you are happening...to life. You are preparing and planning for the experiences that will provide meaning, always realizing that the most difficult part is at the beginning. It's the hardest part. It's the most unpredictable. It's the most uncomfortable. Then...your life is as you dreamed it would be.

Life Management for Meaning

Let's start with the easy stuff and move to that which has been hidden....

1) There are 24 hours in each day.
2) There are 36 hours of demand in each day.
3) Those that demand your time are in conflict with each other.
4) Those that demand your time, each believe they are worthy of being priority #1 in your life.

And as if that weren't enough already . . .

5) No one gave you a rulebook for figuring out what to do and when and how to decide what matters most.

6) When they gave you a system in the past it created more conflict among those in demand of your time.

Your previous system was a failure because . . .

7) It didn't account for the demands of others that matter to you.

8) It didn't recognize that you must take care of emergencies when they arise, and that they arise OFTEN.

9) It didn't take into account what happens if the emergency takes more than a few minutes....what if it takes a few MONTHS?

10) It used an ancient form of goal achievement that never accounted for breaking earth's gravity...it is now outdated because we live in a different world than we did in the Industrial Age.

11) It was stored online...you had to be on your computer to use your system...to know what to do today, the computer had to be on and on your daily planner.

12) It was in a planner that blocked everything out by the hour and then by the quarter hour.

And then there are the more difficult-to-face reasons you need effective time management....

13) No one told you that you had to write down your REAL GOALS and not what would look good if someone saw your planner by accident!

14) No one told you that *if what you write down isn't matching what is in your head as far as goals, then the system will crash instantly.*

What's more . . .

15) You can't predict HOW MUCH TIME SOMETHING WILL TAKE TO ACCOMPLISH.

16) You can't know how you will FEEL while you are doing the tasks involved in various projects...and it can't matter when you do find out!

The real you shares a lot in common with everyone else . . .

KEYPOINT: Always do the projects and work that matter most to your entire FUTURE FIRST each day.

---

17) Our brain is set to STATUS QUO and has no interest in leaving its very NARROW COMFORT ZONE.

18) People are terrible at self-regulation. People aren't "self-starters," they don't continue and rarely, if ever, finish.

19) People only have so much self-discipline bottled up inside for use each day. Once gone...it's gone and tough to get back until tomorrow morning. This one fact is one of the biggest contributors to failure.

20) There are many more obstacles in your quest for your own life than people. There is also your Self. There is the environment and there is the taxman.

So what does all of this mean in real life? It certainly all seems like a big challenge!

- It means that you have a life you want to live.
- It means your life will have meaning.
- You have someone inside of you that you want to be, "you."
- The world has someone "it" wants you to "be."
- Those two things are constantly in conflict.

You already know it, but for simplicity sake, here is your current life script:

1. You want something or some stuff in life. You want to feel something good, get rid of feeling something bad, and you want to have meaning and significance. **No one ever told you about breaking orbit.**

2. You generally can **point to what** those things are that **you want** and have a hint of what would give your life meaning and significance.

3. You can generally **write down those things** (and we will in the future).

4. You can generally **devise a plan** or strategy to move in the direction of those "things."

5. Then stuff **goes wrong** in various parts of life.

6. Some of it is your fault. Some is the fault of the person you live with. Some of it is your boss' fault. Some of it was a random act of "God." But the key fact is BAD STUFF or **UNPLANNED STUFF**, HAPPENED.

7. Now you have **COMPETING COMMITMENTS**. The Daily Planner says to do X but life has just thrown a Q (Someone decides to invite you to their wedding) or a Z (someone dies, gets sick, the neighbor kids egged your car, or you get sick perhaps) at you, and you either have to let X go or you have to do it while navigating Q or Z.

8. You'll have to clean the car, get well, go to the wedding (or not) **AND** get X done.

9. That causes **OVERWHELM** and **STRESS**.

10. That raises levels of **anger, resentment, hostility, frustration** and generates feelings of **blame, guilt, shame** and all kinds of other nonproductive ...stuff.

11. You become **difficult** to work with/live with and your relationships are compromised.

12. It now takes **additional time** to repair what your emotions AND the emotions of others have mixed into the life cocktail. Now X doesn't get done and neither does Q or Z.

13. You all but toss the Daily Planner aside and recognize that **Time Management in its traditional sense simply doesn't work.** (And it doesn't.)

14. You go through life day-by-day, then month-by-month and YEAR BY YEAR missing out on number 1 and 2 above. There is very little meaning, very little significance. There is a minimum of good feelings and sadly plenty of **stress** and **angst**.

15. That's how your life currently works.

And I'd like to change that now...if it's OK with you...

Kevin Hogan

Chapter Eight

Bridging the Forced Life to Your Desired Life by Re-Shaping Your Mindset

G et clear about what you want!
I have a goal. My goal is to show you how you can develop the focus and courage to reach ever-higher levels of achievement than you've ever accomplished before. To live a life rich with meaning. To succeed.

Success, achievement, and meaning are in large part processes that begin and end in your own mind. While your actions and outer circumstances obviously have a huge impact on your success, success is not so much about "what" you do, but HOW you do it.

Lots of people go to work or "try" to make a sale...that's not the deal. The deal is HOW you do those things every day. If you change your actions, you will change your results. If you change your thoughts, you will change your results. Change both today and achieving most things is within reach of most people. Let's get remedial for just a moment.

The first step is to figure out what you want to be successful AT. What do you want to achieve? What do you want to do? It is possible to become successful at nearly anything you do. In fact, you may know people that seem to have a magic touch - practically everything they do is a roaring success. Like David Copperfield, it is an illusion that there is such a thing as a magical touch.

People who do just about everything to the end of success or achievement simply understand the link between actions, thought, plan, contingency and adjustment.

They seem to effortlessly attract amazing opportunities, while others brood jealously from the sideline. They have no trouble making whatever amount of money they choose, while others live paycheck to paycheck.

THINK OF THIS: People who **understand 'action, plan, think, contingency, adjustment'** can start with zero next to anyone else and move to the finish line a winner at just about

115

anything...and they will move quickly, effectively, and make it appear effortless.

Why? They have a genuine drive or passion for what they are doing and the PROCESS of doing it, while others feel lost and confused. How do they do it? What do they have that the public doesn't? It's not as amazing as you might think. They know who they are and what they really want and they don't mind dealing with six weeks of discomfort to experience a lifetime of excellence! Even though I just confirmed it's possible to become successful at almost anything you do - it is MUCH MORE LIKELY that you'll become successful at something you truly like to do.

In fact if you think about the things you like to do, think about doing them or something similar and getting paid a lot of money for doing that. You might think, "Oh you can't get paid to travel and sit on the beach, Kev...."

Really? I know people who do just that. How do you get paid to do what you love? For real...

KEYPOINT: What are the things you like to do and would do daily especially if you got paid what you are getting paid now?

(Remember the things you wrote down earlier?) I'm not really interested if YOU think that this is realistic or possible, I guess I'm more interested in what I THINK YOU CAN DO.

The successful people you meet in life have developed a strong relationship with themselves, become very clear about their passions in life, and made the choice to follow them with enthusiasm, drive, and persistence. They have learned to be uncomfortable doing the unfamiliar and don't have to force themselves to work on their goals each day. It's either habitual or better, **and they look forward to it!**

The results speak for themselves. These people AUTOMATICALLY attract lucrative opportunities, wealth, and even more passionate endeavors to dive into. It doesn't seem like work to them because they are having the time of their life.

Evaluate Your Past Success

Questions: What **goals** have you set in the past, and how did they turn out? Were you successful? Did you make the **decision** to move toward something that wasn't right for you because someone else was achieving success doing the same thing?

> **KEYPOINT: You need to realize that there is no "job security". There is only "YOU SECURITY".**

STOP. Just because attorneys CAN make a lot of money and just because doctors CAN be successful in NO WAY means you should pursue these things.

Did you let your parents or teachers talk you into a certain career because it paid well or offered "job security"?

OK, the thing you set goals toward...How did it turn out for you? You may notice something important as you complete your review: even if you were able to achieve a certain level of success at something, it didn't matter if you weren't happy doing it!

The First Thing You Need to Remember About Success and Living a Life Rich with Meaning is that it is NOT About the Money.

Money is just paper. (Well, at least prior to 1972 when the United States was on the gold standard where dollars were actually real money...in those days, money was ....money. It was worth something.)

That isn't the case anymore. Today money is an illusion and a belief (or as close as you can get). Oprah goes on TV, talks for an hour and earns roughly a million dollars that day. John Doe goes on TV that same day and talks for an hour and earns $200. What's the difference?

One is perceived value. One is connection. Another is belief. Another is reputation and credibility...in fact there's a lot of stuff that goes into getting paid a specific dollar figure.

The best answer is that John prepared years ago, asked for and accepted $200.00. Oprah prepared years ago, asked for one million and accepted that. Now just because you or I ask for a million to be on TV today, in no way means we will get that. The difference is that Oprah knew she would ask for a million for TODAY, *10 years ago,* so *she did all the things necessary to be ready to accept one million today.*

A baby is born today. That is not the result of something that happened today. It's the result of an event that happened about nine months ago. **YOU GET PAID TODAY FOR WHAT YOU PRODUCED NINE MONTHS, or maybe nine years ago.**

Do What You Love?

The true essence of success is doing what you LOVE or what brings you the REWARD of MEANING.

Prosperity is a naturally occurring BENEFIT. Successful people are that way because two years ago, they liked what they were doing and knew that if they got better at it and if they became the best, they would get paid for the work they were doing...then...in two years or three years.

A big part of success is understanding the success time horizon. Time horizon is all about planting, harvesting, repeat, repeat and THEN get paid. If you need to get paid NOW, you will never be successful. You MUST want to get paid in TWO years for what you do today.

I opened the mail yesterday and my book *The Psychology of Persuasion* translated into the German language was staring me in the face. Today I opened the mail and found...*The Science of Influence* book translated into the Thai Language...staring me in the face. I wrote *The Science of Influence* 4 years ago. It pays me today. Think like that and you will be successful.

Need to get paid today? Stay in the hamster wheel.

If you want to achieve, take some time to get to know yourself. Figure out what you really feel passionate about. Determine the kinds of things that would be rewarding. Don't look only at the activities themselves, but the underlying essence of what they involve. For example: you may love sports, but you're not really sure why. Look at the various aspects of sports-related activities and consider which of them appeal to you most. Do you love the thrill of competition, the challenge of strategy, the spirit of teamwork - or perhaps the sense of accomplishment that results from honing your mind and body into a fierce athletic machine?

When you understand what you feel passionate about, what you really want, and WHY, you will be heading in the right direction. Sounds sooooo easy...but HOW do you do it?

Plotting Your Course and Planning Your Strategy

Are you feeling a bit clearer about what you REALLY want to be/do/have? If not, take the time to get clear about your passions and what will be worth your lifetime. Be sure, it is time well spent!

Once you have an objective in mind (whether it's a new career path or a personal goal), you need to figure out the simplest and most effective way to achieve it.

> **KEYPOINT: You can't get where you want to go if you don't KNOW where you want to go!**

That means creating a solid plan, identifying key action steps, and planning for the unexpected and your contingencies when the unexpected happens. **It means having a system to MEASURE whether what you are doing is going to contribute to the project succeeding.** Otherwise you can end up doing Q for years and get nothing from it.

STEP ONE: Evaluating Your Self

Everything you build in life needs a foundation. Whether you're constructing a physical building or a new attitude, you need a solid base upon which to build.

If your new goal is to create a lucrative career as a professional singer, you need to know IF you should start in the first place, and then where to start. You might ask yourself questions like these:

- Do I have the image necessary (young, attractive, unique)?
- Do I already have the skill and talent needed?
- Do I need formal training?
- Am I good enough to be a professional singer?
- Do I have any connections in the music industry?

AND THE KEY:

- How can I get my music out there so people will know about me?

The answers to these questions will determine what you should work on first. And maybe, determine that you should NOT pursue this path.

STEP TWO: Identifying Specific KEY Action Steps - and Taking Them!

There are a lot of people whom I don't coach, but that are still friends, people I'd like to see succeed. They start a business or are working on their success plan but they are only running on a new treadmill that goes nowhere.

What are you doing? "Working on my website."

What are you doing to your website? "Cleaning it up, making it look nice." Destined for failure.

What are you doing? "Working on my new business."

What are you doing with your business? "I'm learning more about my product."

Did you finish contacting all the business clubs in town and setting up speaking engagements?

"Tomorrow." Destined for failure.

What are you doing? "Organizing my portfolio so my presentation is more organized." Destined for failure.

People will do EVERYTHING except the things that will CAUSE them to be successful. There are very, very FEW unique daily actions NECESSARY to achieve and have the life you choose, but people avoid them like the plague! Why would anyone avoid easy things that cause success?

> **KEYPOINT: People would rather spend time making their website prettier or editing something or perfecting something else, or ...anything, aside from true productivity.**

You already know that answer...

People who are new to the Coffee Table business (people who have made less than $250,000 take home in business are new in business) **NEED A MENTOR. They need someone** to point out that they had a hard day and did NOTHING. Once you've broken down your larger goal into smaller ones, you should see a clear series of actions that you need to take in order to achieve your goal. Your mentor will if you don't. One of the core questions to ask yourself is this: **Am I spending 8 hours each day causing possible customers and clients to come to me instead of someone else?** NOT whether they would find a pretty website when they get there. NOT whether you are organizing, cleaning, fixing, learning.

ARE YOU SPENDING EIGHT HOURS EACH DAY CAUSING POSSIBLE NEW CUSTOMERS AND CLIENTS TO COME TO YOU INSTEAD OF THE COMPETITION?

Earlier on, we saw that these steps already have an obvious order. For example, if you have no training or you aren't that good, you are probably in the wrong place. You would be wise to work on those aspects of your plan before you try to get your music out to the public or network with people in the music industry.

Once you set your sight on the music industry, you want to CAUSE FANS TO BUY YOUR NEW ALBUM. PERIOD.

Doing anything else is a promise to go broke. Simply keep things in order, and you will steadily and surely move toward the achievement of your goal. However, be sure you are working on the Strategy to Achieve that counts. Don't let yourself be sidetracked by procrastination or fear and into doing the thousands of things that make it a "hard long day" and cause nothing to happen.

STEP THREE: Planning for the Unexpected

While you're identifying your key action steps and forming a plan to tackle them, you MUST begin to plan on all the obstacles that will pop up - and alternate plans to work through them.

If you want to be a pop singer, my first question is do you weigh 130 pounds or less as a woman and 180 pounds or less as a guy? If not, you have just taken a tough field and magnetized yourself to failure. If you aren't thinking about the CUSTOMER and what THEY WANT TO BUY, you don't get success. Your success is ALL ABOUT SERVING PEOPLE.

The more people you serve and make happy (or the equivalent), the more successful you will be. Here's a good way to do this: consider one step of your plan. Think about the complications or obstacles that will or can arise from taking that step. Then come up with additional steps you can take to overcome those complications. Example: One step of your plan involves getting your music out to the public. You decide that getting a job singing at a local club will give you some good exposure. Dandy.

But what will happen if you can't get a local singing job? By thinking ahead, you can come up with alternate plans, such as building a website with audio clips of your music, gathering other musicians together and renting a space to hold an informal musical event for your community, or researching local establishments that have open-mike nights. *You need to appear before thousands so hundreds will buy your album.*

You don't have to give this stage of planning an excessive amount of thought. **Too many goals are easily derailed and dreams crushed when obstacles appear and the goal-seeker doesn't know what to do, so they do nothing.** They give up. Don't let that be you.

The Power of Beliefs

Beliefs aren't everything, but they are so important that because of them, people ram airplanes into buildings filled with other people. Beliefs do matter...beliefs shape how success and failure will happen, or whether they can happen at all.

That said, there's a lot of stuff I do that I don't "believe I will succeed at" that I succeed at just fine. How can that be the case? If my mentor says, "Go do this," I go do that. I MAKE IT HAPPEN whether I believe I can or not. HE believes I can and THAT is what matters on THIS project.

It took me almost a million years before I figured out that I could change my beliefs or strengthen them by choice. (Usually from proving yourself happily right or happily wrong!)

Of course 21st century BS says you can visualize it, get a good feeling about it, be grateful for it and watch it materialize = Failure rate approaching 100%. Add action to that equation and the failure rate approaches 99%. Follow the proven results in this book and you can turn that around and have a Success/Achievement rate approaching 100%. Why the almost 200% divide?

What is the impact of beliefs? Your beliefs impact everything you do (and more importantly what you don't do). You may wonder what beliefs have to do with anything. They're just thoughts after all, right?

Yes, beliefs are indeed thoughts, but they often determine your conscious mind actions and reactions - and they have the power to hold you back from doing what will make you happy. And beliefs are imbued with emotion, usually raw emotion of which you cannot easily control.

- Actions create beliefs.
- Beliefs trigger and loop with emotions.

123

- Emotions direct the body in which our brain/mind reside.
- Thought sometimes comes into play to save us from the above.

Imagine that you have a belief that you don't deserve to be happy and successful. Such a belief would cause you to non-consciously sabotage any plans you make. Or more likely, such beliefs could cause you to not try at all because you believe it would be a waste of your time and energy. Or worse, "try" once and fail so you know "it" doesn't work. How do you know if you have non-conscious "beliefs" that might be holding you back? (To be precise, the non-conscious mind doesn't have beliefs, nor does it think. It simply acts and reacts based upon behaviors that have been repeated over and over again. And, it moves you in the directions of your desires and away from fear and pain.)

The Foundations for Your Basic Beliefs about Your Self
Quiz: (True or False)

1. When I don't get paid what I'm worth, I ask for and typically get more.
2. I find it easy to make substantial amounts of money.
3. I encounter opportunities wherever I go. It's hard to keep up with them all.
4. I am completely in tune with my passions. I know exactly what I want.
5. I am currently doing what I love and could happily do it forever.
6. I am ready to tackle any challenges that I may face. Always do, always will.
7. I feel fear and I control it by acting until I succeed and have for a long time

These seven things aren't beliefs. They are facts that generate beliefs. You will need to CHANGE the facts in order to generate different beliefs. And if you don't, you will stick with the same facts and beliefs forever. Your non-conscious beliefs and emotions are either driving you or you are choosing what you want with your prefrontal cortex...your conscious mind... The two don't go hand in hand very often.

Changing Existing Beliefs

OK, how do you change existing beliefs? Obviously, **acting in spite of your feelings and beliefs is the single most powerful tool you have.** The other way to change beliefs happens in your mind. You replace old beliefs with more empowering beliefs.

Let's consider this notion as an example: "I am ready to tackle any challenges that I may face." If, when you read that to yourself you feel uneasiness or dread, then you know you have a doubt about your ability to handle challenges. Your job is now to persuade, even coerce yourself that you DO have the ability to handle challenges.

Think back to any challenges you have faced in your lifetime. How did you handle them? Did you buckle down and do what needed to be done, or did you cave under the pressure? **If you can recall even one challenge that you were able to handle and overcome, you have a precedent and solid footing to change your belief!**

You simply need to keep convincing yourself (sometimes hour by hour) that if you handled one challenge successfully, you can handle others. And indeed that is a fact. The more frequently and passionately you can reinforce this concept in your mind, the more quickly your underlying belief will change. The more often you can ACT on the concept, the faster and deeper the emotions imbuing the new belief will be. But what if you can't recall any challenges you've overcome successfully in the past? Is it time to give up?

Given no precedents for past victory, you shift to think about opportunities to tackle a challenge now. Pick one simple thing that would be challenging for you, and do it! That may sound intimidating, but you will surprise yourself as long as you don't let yourself go to bed until it is DONE. Most often, you and I are capable of MUCH MORE than we give ourselves credit for. You won't know until you actually experience it. After you handle even one small challenge, you will feel your confidence growing and you'll be eager to take on more. I kid you not. Little actions in the right area can trigger HUGE CHANGES.

Remember that changing your beliefs is a process but if you keep at it, it won't be long before you start to notice a big change in how you view and experience life. And like so many other things in life, the more often you use this strategy, the better you'll get at it.

Stopping Self-Sabotaging Behaviors

I've written a lot about stopping self-sabotage. Without question, the best two CD programs I've created to deal with this are **Lifestorms** and **The Millionaire Mind**. And yes, I would recommend you pick them up in the www.lifestorms.info and www.wealthpackage.info because this is not an area to do a cursory check on. This is preflight checklist on a jet.

It's NOT easy to stop self-sabotage because it can be elusive. Hopefully by now you are feeling much clearer about what you really want, you've come up with a solid plan to achieve it, and you have been evaluating your beliefs in an effort to build your confidence. Let's look at some common problems that could derail your plans if you're not mindful of them: self-sabotaging behaviors.

Have you ever done something that caused big problems for you and seemed to be in direct opposition to what you thought you wanted? Like consistently shown up late for work even though your boss warned that you were treading on thin ice? Or perhaps you kept feeling compelled to eat junk food even though you were trying to lose weight and get in shape?

Why do you do these things? You would think that setting a goal and creating a plan would be enough to get us where we want to go, right? Obviously not…

Fact: The non-conscious mind is on autopilot.
Fact: The non-conscious mind acts first and you figure out what it has done shortly thereafter, leaving your conscious mind to make up excuses for what "you" have done.

The non-conscious mind can and does actively work against both you and me except in fields and areas of repeated and certain expertise. Then the opposite is true. Even if you consciously believe you want something, it doesn't mean that you will pursue it.

You won't. That's just not how the brain works. The answer usually comes down to a feeling or emotion. Fear....or guilt...or shame....or something close. Take a look at these behaviors and ask yourself whether they have ever derailed your plans:

Here's the remedial version.

- You are on a diet to lose 50 pounds.
- You wake up in the morning ready for the day and your diet.
- You handle things brilliantly all day long!
- You even have a modest dinner.
- About two hours before bedtime, you wear down and break down and begin to eat...eat...and eat...
- When you go to bed, you think, "TOMORROW, I'm REALLY going to do this!"

What happened? The remedial version of self sabotage, of course. Go back and look how easy it was to wipe out an entire day of value.

Your self-disciplined and well-intended conscious mind ran out of gas; and your feelings and emotions took over. Your "need", the hunger in this case, eventually overtook conscious thought and shoved it aside. And so it is with pretty much everything.

Want to sign a contract that will promise that you will do something that is good for yourself? Do it first thing in the morning or last thing at night. That's when people want to change the most. But our conscious mind is only so strong in contrast to the non-conscious mind.

And to be more precise, **the conscious mind is stronger by far than the non-conscious mind but the non-conscious mind has the endurance of a marathon runner while the conscious mind can merely run a sprint...albeit well.**

Procrastination

We've already determined earlier in the book that if you've ever found yourself holding back on doing something even though you kept telling yourself you really wanted to do it, you were procrastinating. You may have felt drawn to watch endless hours of television, or felt compelled to suddenly clean out your basement, or caused dramatic episodes with friends and family members for no apparent reason - all so you wouldn't have to do something that would truly matter in life.

You were trying to distract yourself. Why? Believe it or not, procrastination usually is found somewhere between laziness and avoidance. Most often, you are trying to avoid an underlying fear or resistance that you don't feel ready to handle. (Remember the formula?!)

Habits

No matter how fired up you are about your goals, your old, ingrained habits are as solid as concrete. The biggest mistakes people make are often in underestimating the amount of energy that will be required when we first start making changes.

Doing that which you are familiar with takes little NEW energy and is rarely overridden by anything else. We're used to doing things a certain way and if we try to change those comfortable old routines, we feel nervous and out of place. Part of the survival instinct that isn't all that necessary anymore.

In order to become comfortable with new habits, you need to stick with them long enough so that they become second nature. And that's a lot easier said than done. Remember, that's how you got comfortable where you are now...by habit - even if it's not close to where you want to be.

A significant amount of leverage, action, focus and will is needed in order to change old habits, but once changed, like cement...yep.... they become non-conscious and semi-permanent.

Chapter Nine

The Only Goal Setting System That Works

I t's always been tempting to write a book about the stupid things people say and the stupider things people believe...something like The Darwin Awards.

Here's one of my favorites, "A goal is a dream with a deadline." Nonsense.

Sort of like when the City says, "Yes, this project is going to be done by Johnson Corporation and will be completed by June 15, 2011." And people actually believe that. Everyone does. "Oh, yeah but don't worry, it will be done by June 15, next year." You and I know differently, of course. But hey, that "dream with a deadline," thing makes for good copy.

Sad Fact: ...once people figure out that dreams don't happen on deadline, they sometimes become disenchanted, frustrated, feel a sense of failure, and worse - they feel inadequate. And there is no reason for any of this.

> **KEYPOINT: If all you needed were a goal and a time stamp, life would be sooooooooo breezy easy that we'd just "attract" everything we wanted effortlessly into our driveway....**

We know it doesn't work like that and it never will. There are a lot of myths about "goal setting." And, there are a lot of goals that need to be set. How do you know what kinds of goals to set and what will actually be the most constructive system to achieve those goals?

I'm going to show you. A dream with a deadline is most likely to remain a dream, or become a nightmare. A dream with a deadline is almost a guaranteed recipe for failure.

"We will balance the budget by 2012." You'll never hear talk of "balancing the budget again," at least not in the United States. You could list thousands of them. Dreams are important to having a great life, but when you start attaching iron clad deadlines on them, you create a lot of problems.

I finished the final draft of *The Psychology of Persuasion* in February 1991, right after Desert Storm. I met that goal. My next goal was to have it in print by January 1, 1993. Had that been a dream with a deadline, it would have been dead! *The Psychology of Persuasion* was published in May 1996. It took five years to find a publisher and get it in print. Five years. Good "copy" doesn't necessarily make for a rewarding life... or best selling books.... What does?

Goal setting as it is typically taught rarely "works." There is, however, a system that is actually likely to succeed with predictability. A couple of thumbnail sketches of success will help reveal the plan...

The Beatles didn't sit down and plan on being the most successful rock group in history. Elvis didn't set a goal to become the number one performer in the history of the world. But they did, and on a per capita basis no one ever came close to touching either of them. (Per capita in this case means percentage of people in a country that bought record albums.)

Achievement seems to work a bit differently than starting with a goal. In fact, **success doesn't necessarily start with setting a goal**. Elvis Presley loved to sing. He cut a record for his Mom as a gift and the studio owner couldn't believe how good it was. Elvis always had just loved to sing. Gospel, blues, country. He did some local events and had a great time. His dream, his goal was to get on the Grand Ole Opry. They literally told him to go back to driving a truck. He had no chance of success.

The intense negative reaction in Nashville hurt the young Presley and motivated him and his backup band to get more gigs, learn more songs and have more fun...and they did. A set of movie contracts tied the young man up for a period of 8 years at which time he once again went back to what he loved. Singing to a live audience. It was then that he realized his real dream. It wasn't to be #1, it was to have fun. While he was on track and having fun, he succeeded richly. When he was off track, his life self-destructed.

The Beatles story was similar. From '60-'62, they just wanted to have fun, keep getting better, write songs, and live a dream. They never planned on becoming #1. All of them were often quoted as saying that they would be lucky to see their success continue another few months. Like Elvis, their goals were largely short-term. Learn more songs, get better as musicians, put out as much good material as they could. And...have fun. While they were having fun, they succeeded. Once other things became more important than the current dream of playing, they bitterly split.

The residual from their work never dwindled and they all succeeded in their new careers as soloists, as we know. **When you analyze those who succeed at anything, they almost always do so by doing something they are either: a) good at; or b) love; or c) both. When you look at the lives of people who live unfulfilling lives, they often have as much skill as those who love their work, but they are not doing what they love**.

The foundation of "goal-setting" is laid in the love of the dream. Is the dream a nightmare, or is it truly a dream? Many people are very skilled, say, as a musician only because their parents made them play when they were children, but they don't actually enjoy their playing to any significant degree. Where there is no desire, there is no passion for the goal.

It's very hard to artificially generate a passion for something you don't love. That doesn't mean you can't enjoy success at it, however. Someone who has a passion for financial independence and the lifestyle it brings, can definitely do something they don't enjoy to achieve that goal. Clearly when one lives a life that one enjoys and one where you are doing what you love while storing nuts for the future .... is superior to any other alternative....so as you think of mid-term and long-term goals, you want to think in terms of doing something that rewards you just for doing it. Something you might do for the love of the experience itself. This is more than just a useful philosophy. This is good neuroscience.

In other words: If you have to try and think about your goal and actually might forget about it from day to day or hour to hour, the goal could be worthwhile, but it is very unlikely to ever manifest in reality.

The vast majority of your brain function operates outside of your awareness. Whatever the emotional and survival elements of the brain focus on, (outside of your awareness)

that is you are likely to be driven to move toward and away from. Your brain will focus on what will fulfill your CORE desires and bring you into a desirable state of being.

$10,000 KEYPOINT: Desire drives emotion. Emotion is fundamental to attention. Attention is necessary for acquisition.

This "state" differs from person to person. Some people need calm. Others need excitement. There is no universal state of being that is desirable for everyone, though everyone does seem to benefit from the ability to be calm at least some of the time.

If you think it would be desirable to become a manager at your company, but you are emotionally being driven away from your work to find fulfillment elsewhere, your goal-setting is going to most likely be met with a lot of frustration even if you are successful.

There are a number of aspects of life in which you can achieve goals. There are a number of careers, jobs, lifestyles you can live with and even thrive on. The first area of true consideration is answering this simple question: What are some of those possibilities?

Here is a certainty: **Where you put your attention is the general direction you are likely to go. If you focus on what you don't want, you may very well find yourself getting it anyway**. There is nothing metaphysical about this....and in fact, when goal setting or doing any planning at all YOU MUST figure out what you don't want. BUT, because you are human, the brain will default to programming vs. conscious control.

Once you have figured out what you DON'T WANT and you have laid out your map with contingencies, then you focus on the map and following it.

And what you DON'T WANT MUST GENERATE FEELINGS of FEAR or PAIN or similar. Again, it's simple science.

At this point whatever pictures you put in your brain are the only pieces of information your brain can utilize to direct the body toward or away. If your response to your fear is phobic, your brain will do everything in its power to move you away from the stimulus.

In these cases, say the fear of extreme poverty can cause you to work hard to avoid poverty. A phobia and powerful fear can definitely move you away from something.

However, when you are thinking of choices that are neither phobic nor which you are passionate about, you have a very different situation.

Your brain will lock onto these images and move you toward them. If there are many different pictures that don't have a common theme, you will simply move in multiple directions.

This may not be a bad thing. If your goals are to be "a little of everything", that is very legitimate and could be very fulfilling.

Most people however, have a sense of dream or purpose. Carve the following **3 Key Goal Setting Principles** into your Tablet of Stone.

3 Key Goal Setting Principles

KEY PRINCIPLE ONE: You are far more likely to achieve any goal if you are truly attached to it in some emotional way. (Does it bring out feelings of excitement, calm, passion, love, joy, intensity?)

KEY PRINCIPLE TWO: Where your attention is largely determines what your outcome will actually be.

KEY PRINCIPLE THREE: Although long-term goals are fine, I am far more concerned about your short and mid-term goals. Put the majority of your attention on the goals that are going to come to fruition (or not!) soon.

Therefore, set short-term goals that you can use to evaluate how your journey is going. (Ex. Are you having fun? Are you learning what you need to learn? Are you seeing how your current activity is directly related to your longer-term success?)

Long-term goals are typically not compelling for most people. Everyone knows they should save $10,000 per year from now until retirement so they can retire with a tiny nest egg, but less than 1% will actually do what they need. They will instead do what they want. Assume that you will do this as well (at least for now!). Deadlines are another thing.

How Failure Creeps Up...

In 1998, I wanted to start a school. Having met some of my life goals (write 10 books, speak internationally, be a good Dad, etc.) I wanted to establish the first licensed school for hypnosis in Minnesota. I had a clear vision of what I wanted to do. I had determined very specific outcomes. Curriculum, location, standards...and a date. I put it out one year. For me that is a long-term time horizon on projects like this. I'm used to moving at lightning speed.

Everything was done at the 4-month mark except licensure. Licensure was to be my last project because I've never been one to enjoy paperwork, deal in the minutia of governmental bureaucracy and well...you get the idea. Surely we could accomplish the paperwork and pay the exorbitant fees for licensure in a matter of weeks. Not a chance.

Oh, the money was all paid up front. The State doesn't accept applications without big checks attached. It was then one year until the state would issue the license. Total time: 16 months. If I moved that slowly in my real life...nothing would ever get done and there would be no life...

The problem with deadlines is that most people come to a deadline, pass it, and then quit. "It just wasn't meant to be"...one tends to whisper. There is so much more to a goal than having a dream with a deadline. Having a plan, a schedule, and a clear picture of the outcome are all critical to success. Then there are other elements including contingency plans and persisting in the face of adversity, among others. Don't lock yourself into an all or nothing date by which you MUST achieve something.

Let's start to apply the first three principles of goal setting. Take your time and enjoy this first process. If it's not fun, then you are thinking about someone else's life! This should be a RICH experience!

Goal Setting for *Living the Life You Want* **:**
Preparation Logging

Do this before continuing to read on...
In your Journal, allow for about 10-20 pages for this project.

1. Think of all **the things in life that are important to you** on every level. Things you want to do, be or have. You could already possess these "things" or you might have just thought of them for the first time! Contribution to society, love, sex, happiness, spending time with the family, doing work you are proud of. Write everything down that comes to mind. Leave five lines below each item for evaluation. Journal this. **Write down at least fifty "items."**

2. In your journal, next to each of these things, write a number from 1-10 (10 being most) in **how much you really want this in your life.** This step is crucial. If you are anything but 100% honest with yourself, you will sabotage the entire process. You can have more 10's than 7's or vice versa, but do your best to evaluate just how important each thing is to you in life.

3. Next to each "item" above, write one or two sentences that explains **specifically how you will measure or know whether you are on track to begin integrating this item into your life at ninety days from today.** If you wrote that you want a yacht, a spouse, a new house...you probably won't have those things in 90 days (at least I hope not). I will need you to show what level of progress you want to experience by that 90-day mark.

This is the genesis of successful goal setting that works.

The Goal-Setting Distinction Between Failure and Success

I'm interested in what people do to succeed. BUT, **the idea that just MODELING ONE PERSON's SUCCESS without**

FACTORING IN ALL THE MODELS FOR FAILURE is DESTINED FOR FAILURE.

What I do and share with those I mentor has an approach that ONLY deals with the facts of what actually works in setting outcomes and achieving them. It begins with studying failure and finding out what caused failure...finding out what makes everyone get a failure result when they "aimed" at the success target.

Then I move to the fact that successful people do a lot of the same things that people who fail do, but there are DIFFERENCES and almost no one finds those differences. And that means the chances of achievement are remote. Period.

One of the biggest problems I encountered in getting results in life was meticulously following the FAULTY ADVICE of people who didn't know a thing about goal setting. They knew how to say the words. They could utter a philosophy that seemed to make sense. It SOUNDED easy. It sounded FOOLPROOF. It led to failure after failure...and I found out over a decade it wasn't just me but EVERYONE who used these "strategies" for goal setting that failed. The advice was poorly conceived almost always based on the experience of a few people.

Almost all goal setting advice was based upon looking at the lives of a few successful people and then distilling that into a common sense approach to goal setting. That sounds in theory like a good idea...except one thing...it works for almost no one. Why?

What happens is this: You tell 100 people to run as fast as they can when they start the marathon. Run and don't look back. See yourself crossing the finish line and the crowd going wild. And guess what? It WORKS for ONE PERSON. Then people who teach goal setting say, "What did he do?"

Then they say, "OH! That makes sense. I'll tell everyone else to do that." Problem is 99 people used the same strategy and failed. But when you interview the ONE, he tells you what he did and it's convincing. It's persuasive. It's even COMPELLING. And for the most part, it's the wrong strategy for most people.

You and I have set THOUSANDS of goals. We followed the advice to the T. We did what we were supposed to do and

THOUSANDS of times we didn't get what we wanted. Once again, THE SYSTEM WAS FAULTY, but it LOOKED GOOD.

Today, some 14 years after the "great aha," I continue to approach goal setting for results very differently from other gurus. The DIFFERENT strategies that people who are "successes" and "failures" use are DIFFICULT to tease out from each other. Both successes and failures use the "old model" of goal setting. The ones who succeed make the paper and tell the strategy that all 100 (or 1000) of the failures used as well. I hate those odds......

One Factor That Helps...

First: Short-term goals are far more motivating and are FAR more likely to be met than long-term goals. This is so important. PLEASE don't just read past this. Almost every self-proclaimed expert purports that you need a long-term goal, a life plan, a mission statement. Theses things are all helpful for some businesses and some people but some of these things might just get in the way of getting things done!

Fact: This is not correct and it leads the 99 astray while the 1 achieves and when the 1 who achieves gets to the front of the room and tells their story, it resonates with the audience in all but one way. The guilt and embarrassment of failure for the people in the audience...because they did THE SAME THING AND FAILED. **When in doubt, stick with short-term goals of less than one year, and preferably less than 120 days.**

One Factor That Hurts....

Second: Many long-term goals are FAR TOO BIG. At first it sounds good. Think: Yacht, beaches, travel, wealth, wine, women (or men, take your pick), happiness. And what happens in most cases?

Devastation. This kind of thinking erodes away at the individual and CAUSES long-term failure and hopelessness. Now, with JUST those TWO facts in mind, here is some pretty amazing new information that I think will help you make next year the best year you have ever had.

What Works in Goal Setting?

First let's go to the part that is necessary for success that the gurus get right. Among surveyed independent salespeople, 6 in 10 do not set outcomes or goals at all! This is very sad because this group of people earns the least among all sales people. 3 in 10 set general earnings goals, and they earn twice as much as those setting no goals. Just less than 1 in 10 set specific goals and they earn THREE times as much as those who set no goals at all.

The facts bear out that specific goals matter most when they are:

- Short-term
- Less than six months
- Preferably shorter than three months and...
- Best if they are even shorter than ONE MONTH!

Now, let's just pause here. I invest a little more than 15 minutes per week in some intentional Outcome Based Thinking. You read about it in *The Psychology of Persuasion*. It's simple but incredibly potent for getting what you want. That's it. 15 minutes. 15 minutes in determining what outcomes will happen this week, what to do in case of unexpected obstacles and the plan that will get you past those obstacles so the outcomes happen with no further goal setting required.

When there are lots of projects on the plate (recording CDs, writing the new book, preparing taxes, preparing for seminars and seeing clients) I invest perhaps as much as 20 minutes per week in outcome based writing and thinking. (Yes. Everything goes on paper, in a specific planner, in a unique way that allows me to get everything I start completed.)

Just do this, and you will perhaps earn approximately ten-fold what someone who is doing everything you do without predetermining the outcomes in advance along with the other 7 steps. (Remember, 15-20 minutes...) Just this ONE activity that becomes part of the Sunday routine like eating breakfast increases income geometrically. Take your income and play with the numbers for a second....

Most people set their "goals" (As an aside, you should know that I don't actually like this word because it is so poorly defined as a "dream with a deadline") once per year...Guarantee: Not gonna work.

When are outcomes achieved? ***Desired Outcomes* (what you want to be the result of your effort) are going to happen when you continually alter and adjust them daily and achieve those bite-size pieces every single day.** The daily alteration process? About one minute. I wish I could tell you it was a long arduous task. And there are days it requires two minutes but I can't recall a time recently that it required more than that.

What is it about "goal-setting" that successful salespeople were found to do that others don't? (My guess is that the results of these studies will cross over to "people in general" who predetermine outcomes in ALL areas of life)

1. First, **setting challenging and reachable SHORT-TERM (today through this week) outcomes BUILDS SELF-CONFIDENCE. When you "write it down," it becomes part of the reality of the external world.** While it is running around your brain, it's just getting tired and will eventually stop running and quit. "Thinking goals" is a general waste of time.

2. Second, **setting SHORT-TERM (today through this week) challenging and reachable outcomes encourages PERSONAL COMPETITIVENESS.** You and I have evolved to compete with ourselves to constantly better ourselves...to constantly learn, be happier and reach for those things that seem out of reach.

3. Finally, **setting challenging and reachable outcomes encourages *INTERPERSONAL COMPETITIVENESS.* Here you set yourself side-by-side with others who are doing the same thing that you are and use them as a yardstick as well. Not only do you excel when you compete with your own standards, you compete even more effectively and achieve outcomes when there is competition.** This competition can be agreed upon (like a sprint or a football game) or it can be in your own scorekeeping system in your mind.

These are the three areas that top performers are attentive to every day, and you CAN easily be in the top 10% if you aren't already. BUT there is a problem. Something is missing. What? You can't begin achieving without self-confidence. Just **how do you build self-confidence in yourself** and others?

Here is the outline:

1. First, you cannot be confident if you don't understand or play the game well. Whatever you want to be confident at doing, **you MUST have a complete breadth and depth understanding of the field.**

2. Second, knowledge alone is the foundation but the actual ACHIEVING process is crucial. **Actually DOING something UNTIL it is done and experiencing the pleasure of COMPLETION teaches your unconscious mind to be successful when you do it often enough.**

3. Finally, you come to a point when these two factors carry you ONLY so far...then you must study what it is that causes the failures among those who are using almost IDENTICAL METHODS are doing wrong. You MUST tease out those fine points because they are the DIFFERENCE. Some of those differences will be "historic" and some will be contextual or environmental and not easy to match. And of course often enough, you can't truly match planning to results and make it replicable with certainty.
    Then, and only then, find the best people in your field and get inside their thinking, behavior and their ACTIVITIES.

Chapter Ten

Getting What YOU Really Want

People have been in the same hamster wheel for so long they have no idea or dreams of what they want to be when they can "grow up again." The vast majority of people obviously don't really know what they want. They haven't dreamed of "what they wanna be" since high school. They thought the selection process was over when they got the job after college.

For one moment they're excited over a particular thing or endeavor. The next thing you know they completely abandon it; either because they lose their interest or because they give up when they encounter a little problem. Those who always change their minds and those who give up easily when the going gets tough can never get anywhere.

Maybe right now you're uncertain. You don't seem to know what you really want in life. In your journal, write down and then answer these questions to pick up the Goal Preparation Process:

1. What makes your heart beat with excitement?
2. What makes you happy?
3. What are you consistently thinking of day & night?
4. What do you want to do for the rest of my life?
5. What do you enjoy doing?
6. What are your obsessions?
7. What things make you jump with joy?

Now STOP; don't race past this. DO THIS.

There is ample scientific evidence that actually **writing something onto paper causes people to a) maintain attitudes and b) cause the outcomes of goals to be achieved.**

To help you out, just follow these steps.

1. Write in your journal, all your possible answers for the seven questions above. Write anything, even seemingly unimportant ones.

2. Circle 5 to 7 "items" that capture and hold your attention. Perhaps they are the things that interest you the most.

3. Evaluate and choose with your heart the best one or two (but no more) things that are worthy to spend a great deal of your time & resources with. The chosen one should really be something that brings out the best in you.

The great gift of life is that you can ALWAYS change later and dream NEW dreams.

Simple Ways to Motivate You

1) The Overwhelming Feeling of Attaining your Desired End.

How would you feel after accomplishing your mission? Of course you will feel ecstatic. You might be shedding tears of joy. Let this tremendous feeling sink in and encourage you to persist despite all odds.

2) The Reward System-- very IMPORTANT.

How would you feel if you've entered a contest, but there are no prizes for the winners? It's not very compelling. The same principles apply to your vision. Reward yourself after accomplishing a goal. Set a particular incentive for every objective. Let's say if you've achieved a particular task, you'll treat yourself to your favorite restaurant. When you've finished a bigger task, you'll go on a vacation. Got the idea? Just set something gratifying to indulge in after completing a certain undertaking.

3) The Force of Connection

If you want to succeed, surround yourself with the right kind of people who will support and encourage you all the way. Be with people who have the similar beliefs and aspirations as yours. Results are generated by this fusion of collective energy from people of "like minds."

That's why I have the Inner Circle. Otherwise, being with people who oppose your ways of thinking may trigger a negative, yet very powerful, kind of motivation.

Has anyone ever said to you that, "You'll never get anywhere," or, "You're wasting your time with what you're doing?" Didn't it make you furious and determined enough to prove to them how wrong they were? This is what I'm talking about. When aggravated, you will do anything to make those who are against you swallow their words. This has OFTEN been the best driver of all for me. Perhaps you can use others criticism of you in the same way....

The Component of Confidence That Causes Success

QUICK FACTS:

- You will only do what you are confident that you can do.
- You will only accomplish what you are confident you can accomplish....and...
- You can accomplish a great deal as long as you have unshakable confidence.

Most people out there have a very different idea of what confidence is. They think that if they can talk themselves into believing that they can do something, then they can actually do it. That isn't confidence. That's a smokescreen.

Confidence is this: "I'm going to get that book/article/website/project done before Friday." And, it is done before Friday.

NOTHING would get in the way because you have trained yourself that real world certainty comes from accomplishing what you say you are going to do. THEN, when someone says, "Are you confident you can handle this?" Your response will be:

A) "Heck no, but I'll bust my butt trying, working overtime off the clock until shown it's not possible." (That's a good, rock solid answer.)

B) "No, I can't - give it to someone else." (That's a good, rock solid answer, too. UNDERSTANDING YOUR LIMITATIONS is a GODSEND to the world.)

C) "It will be done before you get here Friday."

Those are the three answers. There is no, "Oh yes, I can do that," and then it doesn't get done. That person needs to get fired....yesterday.

A baseball player will get a hit about 25% of his attempts. He can tell you, "Oh yes, I'll get four hits today", but the fact is that the chances of his getting four hits are 4 to the fourth power, or 4 x 4 x 4 x 4 = 256. He'll go 4 for 4 once every 256 games he comes to bat four times. Twice per season if he plays every day. So, I don't want to hear, "I'm going 4 for 4 today." You want your business plan and your INCOME this year based on a 1/256 chance?

Me too neither!

The answer is, "I'm feeling good. I'm going to go bust butt, make every pitch count, swing at the good pitches and hustle running the second every ball is hit." Or, "No. My leg is screwed up and Johnson will do a heck of a lot better job than I will today."

REAL confidence is obviously weighted with honesty, certainty, and reality-based-thinking (RBT). "But Kevin, shouldn't people just say they are confident so ....fill in the blank with a stupid reason....and a result they want here...."

NO!

"Hi, Kev. I'm your pilot today. Those three drinks I just had at the bar will help me fly better. I'm sure of it." No thanks, there is a clear and distinct line between confidence and abject stupidity.

Strategies to Lift Confidence

227 pounds. February 3, 2004.

It was scary one week later when I saw the videotape of the presentation I gave. The presentation was stellar...really. The focal point in the frame was not. I had gained 30 pounds in 2003. I paid no attention to my weight. I was back into size 40 pants. I was now divorced, disgusted, disappointed, disoriented and every other "d" word you can think of.

For me, and actually for most people, my body weight is all about the volume of what I eat (calories) and keeping track of those calories in advance of what I'm going to eat. I'm not a "work out" kind of guy. My idea of a workout is typing or talking faster. (OK, I do take a walk every day, cut the lawn every week in the summer, shovel in the winter and do gardening and the YUK shrubs....heckuva lot better workout than weights and leg presses...and stuff gets done.)

There is only one way I can lose weight, and it's precisely how I first did it in 1997 when I was 225 pounds and within one year dropped to 188. I knew I had to do something where I would be accountable to my toughest critic. Me.

Each day I would write down the calories/food I was going to eat **before** I ate. I would record faithfully, every day...for a long, long, long time. I didn't know if I could do it in 1997...until I did it. I have a voracious appetite. Weight loss was never something that I had successfully dealt with...but this worked. Each day I wrote down the number of calories I was going to eat before anything went in my mouth. Never in arrears.

That's how Enron went broke and fat people get fatter. I knew I had to take responsibility in advance. Be honest to myself. It would be a long journey. And one year later, I was at 188. I took 37 pounds off the body and I was in size 34 pants. Then about six months after hitting 188, I thought, "Hey, I don't have to keep these daily logs any more..." And then 18 months later I was back in the 210 range...again.

And once again I found my "Achilles heel"...in the mirror... It's so easy to put food in your mouth. It takes a bit of accountability to keep it out of your mouth. So, February 11, I began ...again. 227 pounds.

I'll never forget that day when I was 227....all those years ago. I told my daughter the doc wanted me to drop weight or suffer the consequences. She stood up next to me, took her hand, put it up to my chest and then brought it straight down...only it couldn't go straight down....it hit my stomach. The hand stopped right there. I remember it...vividly.

"You're fat, Dad."

"Thanks, Honey."

I raised her to always be honest and have integrity. (Sigh.) So, I grabbed the pen and paper. Not only did I write down how many calories I would eat before doing so, I would collect the week's total and write the average daily consumption down on the next sheet I would use. It proved to me that since I did it last week, I could do it this week. 211 days later. My weight was exactly 193. Now, that was only a-pound-uh-week...... But hey in 211 days to get 34 pounds off this body....I was happy. Today, I know that when I slack off and don't keep track, that I have the capability to get it together. It will happen because .....it will happen. No visualization, no imagination, it just IS.

Confidence = Commitment + Plan + Previous Accomplishment + Determination

When you set a goal, decide on an outcome, predetermine your result, you must be accountable to yourself, the record, and preferably to someone else. Someone whose opinion matters. Someone who can praise you when you succeed and get on your case when you start to lose.

In fact, if you are going to be a little embarrassed when you tell the person you are accountable to that you screwed up or "failed," then you have the right person. And if you can't tell that person that you "failed," then you don't need to start in the first place. Your commitment isn't there.

Accountability is the Key

As soon as you decide to be accountable to any or all the above, you have made the first step toward experiencing unwavering self-confidence that IS commitment, plan, previous accomplishment, driven by determination.

Every week, people decide to go to the store and get groceries. They decide to put gas in the car. They decide to take a shower, go to work and do all kinds of things. Then when it comes to something that they really want but has not yet become a ritual (like getting gas when the gas tank is empty)...they fail. Why?

Because they aren't accountable for the actions. No groceries? Kids get upset. No gas? Your boss gets upset. You don't get paid. No shower? No one you want near you...will go near you. You are instantly accountable.

But starting your own Coffee Table business so you can live the life you want? Doing something that will actually create a life you want to live? There is no accountability. No one notices. No one knows you want something special for YOU. So, you safely let it go. Safe from everyone else, but not from yourself.

Your confidence shrinks. You don't want to create a life. You want someone to "give" you a job. Or you see the protester in the streets instead of at the job interview. You see the person "on strike" instead of in a class where they can learn to be responsible and accountable to themselves.

FACT: Accountability is on the other side of the spectrum from entitlement.

The reason people want to believe they are entitled to something is because they have zero self-confidence to be accountable. No accountability = Failure. People ask me all the time, "How do you create all those programs and write all those books?" Answer: I read thousands of articles, books, monographs and experience life as well as "spectate it."

"No, how do you DO it?"

"Oh. It's like having lunch. You don't think about it. You just do it. It's like kissing your kids good night. You just do it. If you don't, you'd feel terrible."

"No, how do you do IT?"

"I don't go to bed until IT is done."

"What if you get writer's block?"

"I don't let myself get writer's block....it's too much like constipation."

"What if you run out of things to say?"

"That's impossible. The fields I work in are evolving at light speed. The competition is sleeping and I'm moving at the speed of light with the field. I won't put out rehashed work. It's what is happening and working today...there is no other alternative. Be the best or why play?"

"But what about vacation??"

"I'm doing what I choose to do, where I want to do it. I refuse to do otherwise unless it is absolutely necessary (bookkeeping/paying taxes). Isn't that what a vacation is after all?"

New scientific findings come out in the journals every quarter. The Science of Goal Achievement (anyone can SET goals) is tallying up more results.

For example, just recently we learned that if you want people to actually change their behavior, you must get them to see themselves achieving a goal or result, not just seeing that someone else can do it, or stepping into their shoes. That was a surprise.

The "Third Person" Perspective

Now there is more. One of my favorite researchers, Thomas Gilovich, has found some groundbreaking research about "what perspective to see yourself from" if you want to cause change in your behavior, or that of others. The research is useful not only in influencing others, but making the process of changing yourself more likely.

Trying to lose weight, be less nervous when speaking publicly or improve in some other way? One strategy that can help is to switch your point of view from the first-person to a third-person perspective when reviewing your progress, according to a series of studies conducted at Cornell University.

Re-Framing Influences

"We have found that perspective can influence your interpretation of past events. In a situation in which change is likely, we find that observing yourself as a third person -- looking at yourself from an outside observer's perspective -- can help accentuate the changes you've made more than using a first-person perspective," says Thomas Gilovich, professor of psychology at Cornell. When people perceive change, they get some satisfaction from their efforts, which, in turn, can give them more motivation to keep on working toward a personal goal, he says.

Gilovich and former graduate students Lisa K. Libby, Cornell Ph.D. and an assistant professor of psychology at Ohio State University, and Richard Eibach, Cornell Ph.D. and an assistant professor of psychology at Yale University, conducted a series of studies to examine the effects of memory perspective on perceiving personal change. Their work is published in The Journal of Personality and Social Psychology (Vol. 88, No. 1, 2005).

The social psychologists asked participants to picture a particular event from their lives either from a first-person or third-person perspective. The volunteers then evaluated how much they thought they had changed since the event had occurred. For example, in one study 38 college students who had been in psychotherapy were asked either to recall their first appointment through their own eyes (first person) or "from an observer's visual perspective" (third person). Those who recalled their appointment from a third-person perspective reported that they had made significantly more progress in treatment than did those who took a first-person perspective. What else did researchers uncover? The researchers also found that memory perspective can affect behavior.

They recruited college students who said they had been socially awkward in high school and asked them to visualize an occasion of their social awkwardness either from a first- or third-person perspective. **Not only were those who recalled their awkwardness from a third-person perspective more likely to say they had changed, but they also were more likely to be**

more socially adept -- initiating conversations, for example -- just after the experiment when they did not know they were being observed.

"When participants recalled past awkwardness from a third-person perspective, they felt they had changed and were now more socially skilled," said Libby, the first author of the study. "That led them to behave more sociably and appear more socially skilled to the research assistant."

Gilovich points out, however, that a third-person perspective accentuates perceived changes when people seeking self-improvement are focused on differences between their present and past selves. But when the volunteers were asked to focus on similarities from the past by visualizing a past event that was positive, such as something they were proud of, the third-person perspective tended to promote perceptions of continuity between the present self and a positive past self.

"In other words, recalling memories from a third-person perspective produces judgments of greater self-change when people are inclined to look for evidence of change, but lesser self-change when they are inclined to look for similarities from the past or evidence of continuity," concluded Gilovich. The research suggests that the saying, "It depends on how you look at it," has literal truth when it comes to assessing personal change.

Chapter Eleven

Time for A Change: Shifting from Overwhelm to Productive

Y ou now know that the goals that were once set can be re-set so you can actually attain them.

You now know that procrastination can be beaten. You can do it.

You now know that it requires quite the slingshot effect to break free of earth's gravity. You know its three stages; and the first two require 96% of all the energy in breaking free...to freedom.

You now know that you CAN live the life YOU WANT. But I bet it still seems a bit like a dream.

The Great Equalizer

Time....

Regardless of the cards you are dealt in life, the one constant is time. Depending on your cards and choices, it might seem that others have more time than you do...and they don't.

Earlier in the book you found out about "life currencies." People argue what's more important in life, money or love. Without money you can't feed, clothe, shelter, and protect the ones you love.

But without time, you can't give love.

One of the reasons that you are most likely to lose your spouse to the guy or gal at the office is because that's where he spends most of his time. If you want to compete with the time that person is getting, you need to have created some spaces of your own.

And the three are arguably currencies that we trade off in differing degrees. In other words, we trade money for time, time for love and love for money. (Not necessarily in a romantic sense but in an evolutionary sense.)

Time is also one more thing...it's the core life commodity.

You can fix things you've screwed up or get different cards for your lot in life. But...you cannot go back to relive a moment in time, and you cannot jump forward in time.

All you have is right now, and if are not using the time you have to live your best, most effective life, you will very shortly feel stressed.

BUT...what IS the best, most effective life?!

The smart person realizes that they are going to have another 365, 7000 or 15000 days left on this earth. You could argue that the smaller the number of days you have remaining, the more important they become to you.

When I created *Time for Love, Time for Money*, part of my intention was to show that time management is sometimes, but not always a bit of a misnomer. Time production, creating time for things you want or need to do is really one key. The other key is that **when people talk about time management, that's code for Self Management....but maybe not in the way you think.**

Time management is not necessarily about setting rigid schedules, but it can be if you are in the corporate world and at the beck and call of appointments. And if this is you, you do need to master scheduling. I'll offer some tips about this later. I'll also show you a way to utilize your planner for this kind of lifestyle in the resources section at the end of this book.

Why Are You Overwhelmed?

As you live in the middle of a chaotic life, you may wonder how you got here. Where did you go wrong? When did everything get so out of control? How did you end up with so many responsibilities? Most importantly, how can you get back on track without having to ditch your entire routine and start over?

You try to be a good person, to have time for everyone, to do your best and help others as much as you can. You try to be supportive to your family members, friends, co-workers, boss, but somehow all of your good intentions get tangled up into a big, soupy mess.

You find yourself agreeing to things you really don't want to do, adding more and more items to your, frankly, ill-created To Do List, and racing blindly from one task to the next in order to get everything done on a daily basis.

Despite your best efforts, you almost never accomplish everything you want to get done, so you start making sacrifices to try to squeeze out a little more time. Perhaps you reduce your self-care time or avoid social gatherings because you're just too stressed or drained to have a good time.

So What is the Answer?

KEYPOINT: Part of the solution is to say, "No," in a kind loving and gentle fashion.

If I said, "yes" to everyone who wanted to talk for "just five minutes," I wouldn't be able to see. If I accepted every luncheon, I'd weigh 400 pounds.

KEYPOINT: You MUST say "no" a lot more often and create your day around what you want and need to do.

Most people spend years not doing something they regret later.

They don't keep the house up. They don't give their kids time.

They don't plan an appointment with their spouse today. Don't plan an appointment, and your marriage will explode or wither. Remember life is all about time and where and with whom it's being spent.

So, why all the chaos and craziness in life?

ANSWER: Too much to do in too many different "parts of life."

LIFETIME KEYPOINT: People are involved in more activity that has no outcome other than guilt reduction than at any time in history.

If your schedule is crammed full of obligations that simply MUST be done on a daily basis, you will undoubtedly begin to feel that you just don't have enough time in the day. Between work and family obligations, community commitments, favors to others, errands, and numerous other tasks, you probably feel that squeezing in "one more thing" will make the whole thing explode from the pressure (and you along with it!).

So STOP.

Think about what that means.

When I do "live" events at corporations around the world, I almost always tell the story of my Mom...

Got up in the morning. Got the five kids ready for school. Went to work. Got home about 5:30 or so. Started dinner. Cleaned while she cooked. Kept the kids in line. Cleaned more. Did more laundry. Took care of the baby. Went to bed.

Mom wanted those kids, but she also wanted someone to be there to help out as part of the parent/worker team. Instead, like so many families, she ended up doing it all.

No wonder she could be a pain to live with. She was IN pain.

Don't get me wrong. She loved her kids. Loved having them around.

But when someone leaves you and the next guy dies, you have a big WOW problem and something you didn't plan for.

And that was Mom's big mistake.

She lived as if hubby #2 would stay and hubby #3 wouldn't die not long after.

Mistake?!

How can you plan for someone leaving?

How can you plan for someone passing away unexpectedly?

Lesson One in Self Management: Your life today is going to become MUCH MORE complicated as time goes on.

People do NOT plan for divorce. They don't plan for the death of a spouse or a child. They don't prepare for the four-year hospitalization and when they happen (and they WILL happen if they haven't already) the family is left with an almost impossible life to live.

Mom was great in the moment. She was great under fire. She handled crisis after crisis. There were a lot of them.

But *NO ONE taught her how to prepare for all of life's crises financially, psychologically or emotionally.*

A KEY COMPONENT OF SELF MANAGEMENT is to remember that right now things are as easy as they are going to get.

If you are a manager at a corporation, understanding this about your life and that of your employees will give you a complete paradigm shift that will help you run a productive and profitable office where people not only respect you, but will work their butt off for you.

Research shows it's human nature to think that "things will get better," that they'll have "more time." But they don't and they won't.

A BIG, BIG, BIG PART OF SELF MANAGEMENT is to have a CONCRETE PLAN for when the spouse leaves or dies (roughly the same thing) or when the child dies or when the other child is hospitalized.

Because these things happen in pretty much everyone's life, a quality plan needs to be in place. Part of that is preparing, for example, for a few years of no income.

Mom failed to do that, too.

Had she been 10 years younger, she would have. But she was born AFTER the Great Depression. People born BEFORE the Great Depression learned to **prepare for rainy years.** When it rains, it rarely rains for a day...or a month...or "six months." When it rains, it hurricanes... But people HEAR "rainy day" and the metaphor drills into the unconscious that all that's coming is a bad DAY...big deal.

"The two-year plan" **is a necessity**. It doesn't mean you have to have two years of income stashed in the safety deposit box (though that is a very, very good idea), no, it's about the Coffee Table Business you will implement immediately upon the disaster beginning. Because being SIO+K will finish most people, leave only despair and razor thin hope. **(SIO+K= Single Income with One Plus Kid)** We'll talk about that next time.

155

How does culture dictate Time Management?

Unfortunately, in our society there have always been stupid guilt rules about how and what has to be done. Don't work and take care of kids? Wimpy woman. Be better than a man. Work all day, work all night, implode. Most people CAN do the activity and work of several other people...for a time. And then you end up in the hospital.

KEYPOINT: Do NOT let society and culture run YOUR LIFE. PERIOD.

MAJOR LIFE EARTHQUAKE GENERATOR: Conflicting priorities x Wimpy response to social/cultural rules = Disaster

The Earthquake Generator

There is usually an earthquake looming around the corner. But before we go there, let's look at a few simple "self management" factors that might be out of kilter and are actually quite easy to fix.

Maybe your self-management challenges are a lot easier than most. Perhaps it's not that you have too much to do - but too much at specific times. Perhaps you have overlapping deadlines in your work so you have to cram to get everything done on time, or you don't think ahead before agreeing to do something and then have to rush to keep your promises. Maybe your kids have conflicting activities so you constantly find yourself trying to be in two places at one time.

These situations are EASY to handle. You simply must be able deal with it with backbone. And that will help you create a better self...if you handle it right.

What if you don't? What symptoms of impending "Life Storms" do you have?

Lack of Focus or Proper Planning

Even if your priorities don't conflict with each other, you might

156

find yourself creating unintentional conflicts. You might be disorganized or lack a clear schedule, so you end up taking on more than you can handle or forgetting about a responsibility until the last minute. As a result, you end up walking around with scattered thoughts, feeling like you must be forgetting something.

Blurry Boundaries

If you have a hard time saying "no" to favors asked of you, or if you deal with constant interruptions and distractions at work and at home, your boundaries might be blurred. You may have given the impression that you are always available to help your friends, family members, co-workers, and neighbors with whatever they need.

Have you ever heard yourself say, "Call me anytime. . . Sure I'd love to help . . . I'm always here for you . . ." and so on? Most people are eager to take you up on such offers - even when it's inconvenient for you!

Lack of Discipline

Even when you know what has to be done each day, you may have trouble getting it all done. People get lazy at the end of the day. They go off their diet at the end of the day then decide in bed that tomorrow will be better. They don't get stuff done today and before they doze off, they promise themselves that they will "tomorrow." And of course when you promise your SELF stuff and you FAIL to come through, your SELF doesn't TRUST YOU any more.

Think that might cause long-term self-sabotage...short-term sick days?

You might find yourself wasting time on unproductive activities or avoiding certain tasks because you don't enjoy them. As a result, you berate yourself for not being capable enough or focused enough to be as productive as you want to be. Berating yourself is a waste of your time, too....

You must instantly get up and go DO those things. You must get them done or the mountain of dynamite is getting ready to be set off to generate one quality earthquake.

Failure

Yes, you will fail...people never fail at their "job" because they do the same thing every day. Jobs are like playing catch with your friend. You can throw the ball for an hour and talk the whole time because you've done it over and over.

Anything that has a "success" end result and anything that moves you in the direction of living the life YOU WANT TO LIVE, DEMANDS FAILURE and LOTS OF IT.

Failure is not a judgment on your SELF when seeking to achieve. Failing at your JOB which you do every day for 10 years IS a comment on your competence.

If you don't address your underlying fears, you'll keep putting off the activities that will make you successful - no matter how badly you might want to do them.

Other examples might include:

- Having a lack of belief in your ability to do something, so you avoid trying in the first place.
- Confusion about the best way to proceed so ,you don't create a clear plan of action
- Believing that certain tasks or goals will be extremely difficult so you keep putting them off.

And where did YOU say, "oh man, that's me?

You might recognize a bit of yourself in each of the above habits, but which of them is screaming for attention? Which of them makes you feel like I must be spying on your life?

It's true that you must play to your strengths in your life, but that factoid needs to be "contextualized" to a life experience and situation that can GIVE YOU A SECURE, SAFE, LIFE.

Quick Project

Here is a simple exercise that can help reveal the main reasons you feel out of control:

Grab your journal and a pen. Read the following question and write down the FIRST THING that comes to mind as your answer. Don't analyze it, just answer go ahead and answer.

Exercise - Answer this question:

"My life would be much less stressful if...

and...,

and...,"

What did you answer; and what does that say about your habits?
   Examine your answer very carefully because it holds powerful clues to help you understand why you are overwhelmed! Take a few minutes to jot down the insights you received from your answer, and what you think they mean.

...Maybe you said....

"My life would be much less stressful if everyone would just leave me alone."

If your answer was similar to this, (even if worded differently) it is a clear indication that you feel overwhelmed with demands from other people. Whether those people are your family, boss, friends, community leaders, or anyone else - you are spending too much time focused on other people and not yourself. That means your boundaries are blurred - or non- existent.

Look at this word: **"NO"**

Say it. (Doesn't feel good, does it?)

Say, "No John, I can't come down Sunday and I can't go to church. I'm going to cut the lawn, do some Bible Study and watch the football game." (Or the equivalent thereof.)

...Or maybe you said...

"My life would be much less stressful if I could clone myself."

Obviously, this answer reveals a heavy to-do list and not enough time to accomplish everything on it. If you've ever wished there was more than one of you to get everything done each day, you are probably taking on too much.

Time to OUTSOURCE. Even if it's overseas. OUTSOURCE. And, yes your kids are a place you can outsource to. Your kids don't do 10% of what *you* did as a kid. (True or true?) Let them (cause them) to learn the same strengths that you developed or they are really screwed come age 18, 21, 27, 32...

...Or did you say...

"My life would be much less stressful if I had more time to care for myself."

This answer reveals a habit of taking care of everyone else except yourself. It means you are sacrificing your own self- care in order to meet the demands of others, which only makes you feel more stressed.

I had a client who was a psychiatrist (I needed a psych but she was my client, not my doc!). She had spent EVERY single day of the last 16 years of her life taking care of her paraplegic daughter with almost no ability to move.

I sent her to Disneyland and to a New Age Reiki Master. One week away from her daughter. First time in 16 years.

No, I hadn't lost my mind. I didn't find evidence for Reiki as a healing modality, but the fact is that Reiki Masters put their attention on YOU and only YOU and they are in the MOMENT with you. THAT is worth a lot. As I told the woman, "If you die, no one will be there for your daughter." Dad, of course, left as soon as he found out how hard the baby's life was going to be...oh...and how hard his was going to be because (Go back a few pages), *HE DIDN'T PREPARE FOR A SEVERELY HANDICAPPED CHILD.*

Idiot.

Have sex. Make baby. Leave.

Buddha did it, too, and they say he was enlightened. I always wondered about Mrs. Buddha....

OK, you identified some of your STUFF. Write it down.

What are you really saying with the words you wrote?

It's important to get a clear idea of the MAIN problem before you move on.

(Hey, it's only your life...I mean isn't it more important to call your client back? Screw the phone call. Do THIS.)

As I mentioned, you probably see a little bit of yourself in each of the descriptions above. But at least one of those descriptions will fit you almost exactly (even if the details are slightly unique to your own life).

There is a big difference between being overwhelmed and being productive.

The Productive Person

In everyone else's life, it's pretty simple. People who are productive are worth more. People who are unproductive are worth less. People who don't produce spend their 9-5 at a government building. Almost every time - "management" program starts off with all these things you should be doing and while there is a lot of good information in time management programs, people will always fail if they don't focus on time PRODUCTION. That means producing more time to accomplish what you want to do. That means producing more when you use your time.

How do you produce more? The first answer is, of course, to not be engaged in *anything* that wastes time. Write down what your day was like yesterday, hour by hour. You will be blown away but the number of hours that were useless. And I'm NOT talking about leisure time that you planned in advance. I'm talking about time that simply was blown out of your life for often random "reasons."

161

You have a productive mind, which might be aware that some shifts in thinking are coming soon to a theater near you. See where you are at as you read the following.

THINK: Jobs are abundant for productive people. If you have no job, *make* one. Ever hear, "I can't find a job..."?

Do people believe that jobs are "hidden?" They aren't. Every company on this planet is looking to hire more people to sell their products and services. I don't know of *any* exceptions. There are no "jobs" to "find." They aren't lost. People have this incredible problem in their language-action connection in their brain.

THINK: You can't manage your time until you have some time to manage.

So start by getting rid of wasted time. (No, I'm not going to tell you to turn off the TV. In fact, I encourage you to turn it on and have it on all day. More on this later.) The TV is not at fault. What matters is what you and I choose to do, moment by moment, each day. I want to watch football. I want to watch 24. For me, that's fun. Now if I did ANYTHING "leisurely" all day for some extended period, I'd be moving toward a cliff right? What is happening in your life that is just sucking your life away? What is ripping you of time for YOUR LIFE? WHO is stealing your time? And, gulp, WHY ARE YOU LETTING THEM? And finally, WHAT WILL YOU DO TOMORROW TO STOP THE MADNESS?!

THINK: People who are in meetings all day are not getting things done.

Meetings have their place. I always liked the idea of an ANNUAL MEETING. They are an important way to deal with group issues, create plans and get feedback. I'll be blunt here. I've sat in maybe 5 meetings in my LIFE that were valuable to be at for the people in the room. Almost no one understands how to make a successful meeting happen. The problem is managers want to make their time seem important so they call their employees together without a plan AND OUTCOME. When these meetings start each person has a separate agenda. That is ridiculous. If the purpose is unclear and the participants unprepared are you going to come to a clear and quick decision? If you have to have meetings (and I promise you that you don't)...To avoid wasting time with meetings try the following:

Create an agenda giving each item a time allotment. Prioritize the agenda so the most important issues are dealt with first and quickly. Send the agenda to each participant so they can come prepared. Plan your meeting a week ahead of time...or a month ahead. Focus on getting a solution - scheduling another meeting should not be the solution although it may be a part of completing the plan. (Find the solution.) Avoid last minute meetings. Schedule meetings for the end of the day or week or month or year...so that all involved can arrange their workflow and jump right into their tasks the next morning. If the issue can be dealt with on the phone or through email don't plan a meeting.

THINK PHONE CALLS: You don't have to answer the stupid telephone every time it rings.

Think of this: If you go to the phone every time it rings and your children are safe and sound, you are not a person, you are Pavlov's dog.

Bell: Salivate

Ring: Pick up phone.

NO!

If you have blocked a certain time for working on a task, do not let phone calls interrupt your momentum. While you may feel that you need always be 'on-call' the truth is that you are losing productivity by permitting continual interruptions to your workflow.

Successful people rarely answer the phone. Exceptions? Sure there are. But think of what happens when you answer the phone. You talk and talk and talk and talk. Or they do. Unless you get PAID to answer the phone. Let that baby ring. If you must answer the call and the person can wait ask them for a time when you can call back and discuss the issue. Not only will you set boundaries with your time but also you can be prepared to deal with the call without other distractions. To avoid wasting time with phone calls try the following:

- Turn off your phone for each "half" of your day while you complete your task. If that is too much then do it for one or two hours.
- Ask that your calls be held for the allotted time (making exceptions for those who need it - like your boss).
- If you answer, tell the person you are in the middle of a task so you need to schedule a return call later that day.
- Decide who will make the return call and when.

At my house, there is a rule. If you pick up the phone, YOU have to talk to the person even if they are calling to talk to someone else. It's that simple.

THINK DROP-IN VISITORS: "Do You Have a Minute" will always take longer.

First of all, there are NO drop in visitors. There are people who have an open invitation, and you tell them that. There are people who see you by appointment. There are people who don't see you. Period.

If you cannot finish a task without a co-worker stopping in to ask you for a minute of your time you may find your whole day is occupied with 'one minute' issues. Often the individual will get comfortable and discuss many more items than the one they initially came to you with. Let them hire a therapist. YOU accomplish your work so you can have TIME to be with the people YOU want to be with.

While some positions do require an open door policy, or you may not have an office you can close the door to, it is important to have uninterrupted time in your day to complete the tasks on your list. To avoid wasting time with 'drop-ins' try the following:

- Schedule the time you are not available so YOU stand by your decision
- Close the door or use a 'do-not-disturb' sign to discourage idle visitors.
- If you must deal with a situation or individual ask for the details and suggest you find a time to sit down and discuss it. Schedule it in so they know you view it as important and want to give them your time.

THINK Working at the WRONG TIME: Productive People do not waste resources.

Are you always planning activities that clash with other people's schedules? Do you find the time you allotted to make calls (such as lunch time) means you arc not ablc to gct a hold of anyone? Do you ask for help when everyone else is too busy? Rearranging your schedule to make the most of your time will prevent you from "getting in your own way'. Find the most opportune times for tasks and your day will be much more productive. To avoid wasting time with bad scheduling try the following:

- Do you find more people available to talk later in the day? Make all your return calls then. If people want to talk to you, tell them to wait until after work. Then you'll find they get right to the point.
- Do you often need to ask for assistance with big projects? Plan ahead so that your project does not conflict with other people's schedules.
- Give yourself extra lead-time. Things don't always work out like you plan; give yourself some extra time so you can make your deadlines even if you have setbacks.
- Check up on delegated tasks to make sure they're on schedule and give them early deadlines as well.

THINK Disorganized WORK SPACE. Productive people optimize time and space.

To use your time well it is a MUST that you have an organized workspace. Every moment looking for a pen, a file or a misplaced check not only means wasted time but also it can add to your stress level and interfere with your ability to focus on your work.

To avoid wasting time with disorganized workspace:

- Give EVERYTHING a home. This includes your cell phone and keys.
- Keep daily needs easily accessible. Whether you work from your car or an office, place phone lists, calendars and other daily needed items in an easy to see spot or in an easily accessible folder.
- Put everything else away. Files and tools that are not in use need to be put away. The easiest way to do that is to give yourself at least 50% more storage space than you currently need. If you cram items into a small space you will not likely keep up with your organizing and you will have difficulty finding what you need.

You obviously are aware of other huge wastes of time in your own circumstances. Once you've identified and dealt with key time wasters you will be surprised how much more productive your day can be!

Solutions to Most Time Problems are Found in Short Term Goals:

One of the key ingredients for successfully managing your time is identifying your short goals. And this is where the Daily/Weekly Planner really becomes a useful tool.

Productivity

It usually happens to me in the summer. My brain tells me it's fatigued. It whines and grumbles when "it knows" full well that if it keeps spinning, it stays healthy. If it stops spinning...it probably won't get moving again.

So you crash for an hour and a half and then get back to working position (lying on the couch...oh, the poor brain has it sooooooo tough) and you wake the brain up, out of the hot and humid summer air doldrums.

There are basically two kinds of people in the world that we are living in - those that are productive, and those who procrastinate. In the fast-paced world that we are living in, productivity can be achieved in the snap of a finger. However, if you are slow even to bat an eyelid, someone may take away your golden opportunity to shine in life.

When opportunity comes along, it doesn't come looking JUST for you. It comes and you either seize it, or someone else does. It's as simple as that. ***Productivity's biggest enemy is procrastination or perhaps the government.***

The time/money equation we talked about earlier in the book has never meant more than it does today. In the U.S., people are getting laid off or fired every day because they aren't productive enough to justify their pay.

MESSAGE: Have YOU chosen to be in control of your life?

Businesses of all sizes are looking for good people who can maximize their time and produce results. Every business on the planet is "hiring." The fact is there simply aren't a lot of truly productive (valuable) employees.

Entrepreneurs and salespeople are looking for those results from themselves of course, in addition to those who work with them. In business, procrastinators are useless....and you do not let yourself ever fall victim to the whiney brain.

What is Procrastination? We defined it more gently earlier in the text but here it is without the window dressing:

Procrastination is habit-defeating choice.

...And you and I are fully aware of both the feeling of "whiney" and the rationale that go along with it, versus choosing to be valuable. A lot of time the procrastinator comes up with the most interesting of statements.

"I may not have money, but I'm happy." These two things aren't exchangeable.

Remember we talked about how money and time were exchangeable. Even money and love - or money and sex, in some cases. But money and happiness aren't on a continuum of exchange. Productive people may be happier than procrastinators. They may not be. I don't know. The study hasn't been done. *One thing is certain; there is a LOT less to be SAD about when one is productive.*

The Fears and Failures Surrounding Procrastination and Precluding Productivity

The biggest fear found within the procrastinator is the fear of failure or success. People who are afraid to fail, are fearful of putting in effort or to even try to attempt something. It is much easier to blame failure on their neglecting to complete the task, than on incompetence on their part to do so. Make sense?

Fear of success might seem far-fetched, but there are those that fear change. And **"success" and "change" are often interchangeable terms.** They are "happy" where they are, and while they know that they are capable of building a life, they fear the change in types of work or scope of work that comes with their improved and new capabilities. Hence, they would rather hide behind their apparent level of competence rather than put in the effort and ultimately live the life they want, as they fear being unable to cope with the new workload and expectations. It would be...hard.

Overload and Inability to Prioritize Preclude Productivity

It is very common for all of us to be swamped with work. It is the nature of life that there is stuff to do and it takes significant effort and significant actions to accomplish. The to-do list can feel never ending, and the tasks seem to not stop. The individual fears ever being able to complete anything, if not everything, and is unable to decide which task to start doing. This is similar to an inability to prioritize between the urgent and important, and what is less so.

Also, in high-stress and fast-paced jobs, all the tasks may be urgent and important, and that makes it more difficult because the individual does not know where to start. The person might be scared off into not doing anything. We'll talk more about this later.

Poor Time Management Precludes Productivity

This occurs for two main reasons. First, **people far over-estimate what they can accomplish in a day.** If a person is overconfident in his own abilities, he may risk putting off an important or difficult task to a later date because he believes that with his capabilities, he will be able to finish it in time. This is a common disaster scenario for a lot of people. What happens in real life is there are lots of "emergency situations" that need to be handled, thus leaving little time to do what needs to be done.

Emergencies are something that Productive People count on.

Preparation meeting opportunity is luck. Being prepared for the bad things happening is plain old smart. Because they happen a lot...especially if others are dependent on you. (If one person is dependent on you, you have twice the opportunity for an "emergency." 5 dependents? 5 times the opportunity...make sense?)

Another person might stretch the number of hours available in a day unconsciously. He may plan his time without taking into account fatigue, meals or short breaks needed to keep the mind in tip-top shape.

There are people who fail to prioritize their time effectively. It is always easier to do the simple and unimportant tasks first, but this problem goes beyond that when the individual is unable to differentiate between what needs to be done first, and what is less important.

Boredom Precludes Productivity

An individual may be unproductive because the task is not challenging enough and he feels bored. He finds it difficult to concentrate on the task, and would rather be engaged in alternative activities. This is especially the case for jobs that are repetitive and lengthy, and require very little thought. Not all work is exciting and stimulating, and certain tasks that are repetitive and unchallenging can cause the individual to be less motivated to excel and be productive.

There are a lot of reasons people can be feel bored, it's the response to the boredom that matters when it comes to productivity or what I've come to call "practicing for death" (procrastination).

Poor Self-Esteem Precludes Productivity

There are a lot of people who constantly harbor thoughts that they are not good enough, or that they always fail, and are probably just stupid and incapable. This kind of negative thinking makes it difficult for them to attempt projects, especially important ones, as they feel so inadequate that they should not even be doing a task of this magnitude or importance.

The deal is this: People are as unproductive as they want to be, RIGHT NOW. They are as EFFECTIVE as they want to be, RIGHT NOW. The root cause of this form of thinking could be previous failures, or abrasive and abusive comments from people around them, causing them to be labeled with their own inadequacies and perceived shortcomings.

When people have stereotyped you, USE THAT AS LEVERAGE TO SHOW THEM THEY ARE WRONG. Showing people "how good you are" is fun, showing people they are idiots is, well, intoxicating. In the past, people have underestimated me. Perhaps you can identify.

"He'll never have a successful book...he should get a 'real job'." And then the warp drives kick in.

People who suffer from low self-esteem become unduly affected by people's comments putting them down. They genuinely believe that they are inferior and incapable of working well which is RARELY TRUE. I meet VERY FEW people that can't achieve great things. Unfortunately, believing prolonged condemnation from peers and the people around have caused them to firmly believe that failure is the only thing they can excel in.

Perfectionism Precludes Productivity

Some people have unrealistically high standards and expectations, and this causes them to produce almost nothing as they feel that they do not have the skills and abilities that are needed to complete it satisfactorily. They are afraid of attempting it, and not doing it perfectly, hence they make excuses that they need to acquire more knowledge before they can attempt it. Sound familiar?

The best way to break out of this cycle is to tell yourself that you can do it, and the task is easier than what you think it is. Or perhaps, you need to speak to your supervisor at work to draw up an accurate and realistic level of expectation. If you are a perfectionist, your boss will probably be thrilled to tell you they admire your good work and would rather have you accomplish 100 tasks very well vs. 1 task perfectly.

> **KEYPOINT: It's time to CHANGE WHO YOU LISTEN TO, WHO YOU HANG OUT WITH and WHO YOU BELIEVE IN.**

Enhance Productivity

A) Your first priority is sufficient sleep.

Sure, you'll pull an occasional all-nighter, especially early in any challenging venture. There was a time I pulled a couple of all nighters per month. But that's fine, as long as sleep matters. Most adults need, and I mean need, 7 hours of sleep each night.

I'm not going to stay on this forever, but sleep is crucial to creativity, productivity, clear thinking and good decision-making. You can only go so long with a screwed up sleep schedule before your work suffers. I generally don't sleep but a max of six hours each night, but I often can get a nap in half-way through my day where I can get some REM sleep. And it does matter. Even for people who are getting seven hours each night, a 15-minute break every ninety minutes or so can be a good idea.

How do you know when to break? You break when you have read the same paragraph five times and you don't remember what it said in any of them. Your brain is full, memory loaded and you are in need of a memory dump into your pillow, rebooting the system and coming back with nothing in your cache. (I think we nailed that metaphor, eh?)

So, let's just say 7 hours of sleep each day or night, or whatever. But don't be running around sleep deprived for a week or your productivity will stop as if you were simply being inert again. Simply put, everyone needs sleep but yes, you can have the occasional skipping of 2-3 hours of your sleep but if you turn that into a habit, your lack of sleep will eventually catch up with you and you will find that you no longer are operating at your optimal performance. And no matter how much harder you work, there is a cap to the quality of your work performance.

With this said, I am not enforcing the doctor's prescription of 8 hours of sleep daily with no interruptions and variation of sleeping patterns, rather, it is about knowing what your sleep patterns are. Some people need that solid 8 hours of sleep before they can perform optimally in work the next day, whereas for others, they can do the same with just 6 hours of sleep. Others prefer to spread their naptime throughout the day, taking short naps now and then. The late nights/early mornings may be due to business meetings, product completions or functions or whatever, be it personal or for your business, but you have to remember that health comes first.

B) Handle your own tasks and be you.

What attracts people to run their own business is that they have the flexibility to do whatever they want and whenever they want. For example, even during work, they can take a break and head down to Barnes and Noble to look around and see what is new on the shelves...or simply put on a pair of shoes and go put some pavement under your feet for 20 minutes (sometimes the rough equivalent of a nap for me.)

Entrepreneurs also enjoy a lifestyle where they can get to a doc for a check-up without getting a permission slip from some idiot in a corner office. And maybe the biggest draw of being independent of cubicles is that you can actually get far more done than anyone residing in a cubicle could ever do. The only time I have a "desk" is when I'm on the road and I have to sit at desk in the Suite. I don't like it. It is like a work-stop sign to me. I simply can't be productive sitting at something that feels like an obligation. Give me a pillow, a couch and the laptop and I'm good to go, so to speak. Working how you WANT to work is really important in producing a lot of material. If I'm lying down and typing away, I usually don't feel like I'm working as MUCH.

The other thing is that for some period of time, it's good for you to do your own thing. Outsourcing is great if you have great people to outsource to. And in that case, go for it. I could outsource cutting the lawn, but that's exercise for me and time to clear the mind or think about an upcoming project that I wouldn't get done at the keyboard.

Last year I broke down and got housekeepers. I always thought, "I am NOT too 'good' to avoid cleaning the house." And I'm not. I still do, again, activity that accomplishes trains behavior, BUT when you have too much to do, it's time to call the professionals. I haven't regretted it. Ultimately, the entrepreneur needs help with the biz. You won't be able to run the whole show yourself for long. But two or three people can go a remarkably long way if they are the right people.

YOU need to be doing the stuff that DRIVES YOUR BUSINESS.

C) Master the art of delegation.

The art of delegation, it can be both a boon and a bane. There are people who use it as an excuse to slack off and eventually push away all responsibilities from their shoulders to those whom they delegate tasks to. If you do not take notice, this may eventually happen to you as well. The temptation of shrugging off the responsibilities you are required to carry out may be great, but remember, it is still your business and your family and your life at stake here. Don't be stupid. Delegate wisely.

173

If done correctly, it can greatly help you to free up your time and also optimize your time and capacity. Furthermore, one of the positive things about delegation is that there may be other people who are better at doing certain things than you. In fact...there ARE!

For example, when you delegate jobs to people who work for you, it is evident you would be finding people that are competent in that particular area that you want to delegate to him or her. This way, you not only can free up your time for other things, you also ensure that whatever was delegated is placed into good hands.

- People you delegate to will make mistakes.
- Stupid mistakes.
- And often it will be your own fault.
- You weren't great at training or management.

Doing otherwise is a big fat headache producer. Which brings us to:

D) You are human and remember - they are, too!

It's often hard to accept that fact, but it is very real. Accept that mistakes will happen and do everything possible to ensure that things get back on track and fixed fast. In managing your time, there is one specific necessity....

E) Maintain a *PRIORITIZED* GET STUFF DONE list.

Maintaining a 'GET STUFF DONE' daily list is essential for every successful, productive person.

You need to write this stuff down and you need to line it out when you complete a project, task or appointment. The process keeps you on track and acts as a bit of a reward system as well.

After you have created your own lists and become familiar with The Time Plan System, it is time for you to put them into action. Words or thoughts alone would not produce any significant changes into your current situation and only through acting on what you have planned out can you hope to see a better result in the future.

You do not have to wait for years to see the results, Just weeks or months will do and after which, you can tweak it slightly or modify it after reviewing its performance for that period of time. This way, you can come up with the best plan for yourself and maximize your time and productivity in everything you do.

Especially for businesses, DO NOT cast your plan into stone right after producing it! Business markets are like life itself and are not fixed and are liable to change, and obviously your plan has to change with them! Be flexible when running your own business and you will enjoy your business and your life even more than before. Remember, Time is an Asset.

People in the business world have a saying that time is both your greatest asset and your greatest liability. With each tick and each tock, time passes by and you can never get it back. Time should not be wasted, it should be OPTIMIZED. Make sure that you are able to plan out the best action plan for yourself, and also produce optimally.

- Get your rest
- Take breaks when needed
- Take a walk every day

Get focused on WHAT MATTERS in your business as far as PROFITABILITY. Spend time with the people you choose inside and outside of work. You do that - and you'll not only be productive, but you'll have a good life, too!

Chapter Twelve

Time Plan: The System

I am rarely "busy." I'm usually working on a project. I might be writing a book, recording a CD program, writing an article for *Coffee with Kevin Hogan*, creating an ad or promotion, giving a presentation, consulting, speaking, or researching. Now, when I'm doing one of those things, I'm not busy, I'm working on a project. And there is a difference.

"Busy" means very little is actually getting accomplished. Today I went to the hardware store to pick up an odd shaped light. Then I went to Barnes and Noble, just for the heck of it. Next I popped in at Target and picked up some laundry soap, yard maintenance stuff, some vacuum cleaner bags and some raspberry preserves. Then it was over to the gas station to fill up the gas can for the lawn mower. (I haven't filled the car's gas tank since the snow melted and it's approaching September...no kiddin'....) Got home...and replaced the vacuum bag, scoped out some of the books I lugged home and then dealt with some legal issues that have no upside. There isn't one thing there that was a project. It was all just busy stuff. I got into the world, found people still there and came home.

I could have had someone go do those things and it would have cost me all of twenty bucks to get that done. Instead I lost two hours of project time because I wanted to get out. Don't get me wrong, I made the right decision. I needed to get out. Hadn't started the car since April, so it's nice to know it still loves me. But if I did this everyday, I'd be a "busy guy...." and broke.

Busy people don't get anything done. And this morning I got nothing done. It "felt" kind of good to be out and about, so I probably did my health and psyche some good. All well and good. No regrets. But it could become addictive. Being busy, FEELS like something is getting accomplished when of course in reality, NOTHING of significance is getting done. Go back up to the project list above. That is where my world happens. Busy is like a piece of chocolate. Tastes great...empty calories.

Are you the poster child for "busyness", the one who is never able to get your business projects done (the perpetual starter, then avoider syndrome)? Or even worse, are you the one who has decided to throw the towel because you simply "do not have time"? What I'd like to show you now is the progression of the creation of your time management system to become more productive and achieve your goals.

I really prefer producing or generating time. But let's simply look at managing time...sort of like Time Management 101 for smart people. The key to all this is to focus your efforts on incorporating some simple but profound principles into your life, which are going to allow you to get more done in the limited amount of time you have. I watched hundreds of "busy people" today. Some of them probably thought they were getting something done. They went home exhausted from their shopping and fueling and whatever. For me it was rather exhilarating....

The Tradeoff (A.k.a. Stop the, "I don't have time," Excuse)

The concept of tradeoff is pretty much the notion of giving up something to get something else. No big complicated formula there. It does not necessarily have to "hurt" if you know that it is going to pay off at the end of the day by helping you create a stream of income that will help you achieve financial freedom. This is simply about reprioritizing and giving up unnecessary things and non-productive activities such as spending hours in front of mindless TV shows, sleeping too much, playing video games non-stop, chatting for hours on Myspace or the phone, etc. Two things are common at this point that screw everyone up.

First, a lot of people work on "their goal" and get that stuff done, thinking that everything is cool. But it's not. Working on a goal is not the same as having the rewards IF everything works out. **What's critical is to put your contingency plans into your goal structure and time "management" plan each day.**

Second, a lot of people think that they can't watch *Lost* or *24* or whatever because they have a goal. This is ridiculous. Each week, take 10 hours and assign it to non-goal activities. This can be taking the kids to Cub Scouts, going to church, having the relatives over, watching a movie or going out to eat. Obviously if you choose to cut the lawn, (busy work) then that's the same as watching a TV show. The point is to plan these things at the end of the week for the following week.

There are plenty of non-productive activities that each of us engage in that we could easily give up (or at least reduce the time we spend indulging in them) in order to make our dream of financial freedom or simply a life of freedom, come true. This is a very important. Make the time available by planning non-goal activities at the end of the week...for the following week.

Focus and Intensity

Tomorrow I'll cut the lawn. That's an hour. If I want that to be one of my 10 hours of non-goal activity this week, all I do when I cut the lawn is cut the lawn. But that isn't the case. I'll work on a presentation or plan a product while I cut the lawn. Cutting the lawn requires no thought, so I essentially get an hour of exercise while focused on something that will be extremely important.

The importance of, "I get things done," (Your new mantra) is since we all have a limited amount of time, it is imperative that whenever you are working on a significant task, you give it your absolute undivided attention and energy until it is completed. It pretty much means giving yourself 100% to what you are doing when you are working on your business or anything else that is important for that matter.

I apply this philosophy to all areas of my life and it works without fail. This is pretty much about not approaching your task or project with a *non-committal* attitude and ending up producing some half-a**ed work and results. You can double your productivity just by applying this principle alone. I personally do not like spending an excessive amount of time on any task, so I put all the concentration and energy necessary to get it done in the most reasonable time possible. OK...not always reasonable...fast. Every successful person I know gets things done....fast.

In order to make this possible when you are going to be working during your business time, do not allow any distractions to interfere with your work. That means: NO PHONE CALLS.

Kevin Hogan's Time Plan into Action (A.k.a W.W.K.D.? a.k.a What Would Kevin Do?)

Answer: Kevin would live in the world he created...

Lots of people ask me which daily planner I use. Until I created The Time Plan System I was faithful to no one system. They wanted to know exactly what I do to produce so much material with the same amount of time they have each day and seemingly get very little done. I hesitate to recommend an antiquated planner, but I know you want me to! I hesitate to sell a planner, but I'm going to let you buy one if you like! I can tell you the system I use today is very different from the one I used as a full time, daytime, on the road salesman. At that time I used a Daytimer and if THAT life was my life again, I would incorporate everything in this book right back into the Daytimer daily planner with one page equaling one day of appointments. You have to make some adjustments however.

The problem with this approach was that it ended at 6:00 PM. So from 8 AM - 6 PM it had space for appointments and that was great. Except that life doesn't work on an 8-6. Often you have 7 or 8 or even 9 PM appointments. All that said, for someone with 10 appointments per day, the Daytimer is a good planner. However, you will need a separate planner for home activities because you are literally off the chart at dinnertime! And please don't underestimate the value of everything that happens after dinnertime or before breakfast.

For someone who is more of a project person and not "on the clock" with appointments every half hour, then a project planner makes a lot more sense. Unfortunately there aren't any good planners to fit this bill.

I love many of the planners that are out there but almost all of them fit a traditional businessperson's work style. (9-5, corporate

Check out this web page to see the System Pages I've created for you to use at www.dailyplanner.biz

...and of course, The Time Plan System.

For you...WHICH WORLD WILL YOU LIVE IN?

1) Where you are the master of your life and time.

2) Where you are the slave to someone else's life and time (and it can be OK to be a slave to someone else's time IF they take care of you and you LOVE your work)

3) Where you are not the master, but enjoy and are rewarded for being interdependent with the other person or group/company.

I will look at 1 and 3 as being similar...though not identical.

The two worlds are very different:

Master of Your Time	*Punch the Clock*
Your Time	Their Time
Work	Job
Work til you have a result	Work til end of day
Lose big if you blow time	Cover up if you blow time
Win big if you win with time	Get pd. same if you do good
Try for better, faster, effective	Doesn't matter
Rewarding, invigorating	It's a job. It's ok
Think fast	Think slow
You are free	You are obligated
Don't do things don't want	Go to where I don't want to
Experience no guilt	
Work for me	Work for him

AND they are most different in that you will be productive for HIM and not YOURSELF...and as long as HE is paying your daily wage, that is how it must remain.

W.D.K.D.? What DOES Kevin Do?

- We all have the same # of hours
- We all have enormous stresses.
- We all have people who are sick and dying in our families

181

- We all have tons of problems that could easily stop us from getting a new job, working on a new project, designing a life.

1) I plan my week like this: I **get rewards first**: I get to watch Football, Lost, Survivor. I make sure one night I watch 24. I actively watch about 5 hours of TV each week. I passively have the TV on some of the time I'm home. I have a belief that I DESERVE TO BE ENTERTAINED AND I WILL BE ENTERTAINED. I want to laugh or be fascinated without effort for about an hour per day.

2) I plan to play a game with my son every night at 8 PM (if he wants to) except the evening when The Apprentice is on, and everyone in the house will watch. I plan to spend as much or as little time with my daughter and her girlfriends as she wants to. If they come flitting into the den, I put down my work and talk.

3) I take ZERO phone calls unless I REALLY am required by contract to speak to someone. THIS IS CRUCIAL. The telephone burns up my voice, vocal cords, and steals me blind of time. I LOVE my friends. I have the best in the world but we need to email or talk when I can call back. Same is true for family. I take emergency calls. The phone used to be 3-4 hours of time per day for casual use. You have TWO choices in life. You can talk on the phone or you can get build a safe, sound and secure life. You need to take your pick.

4) NOTICE TO THIS POINT I HAVEN'T EARNED A PENNY. I COME FIRST. When I came second or fourth. Life was impossible.

5) **YOU CAN'T BE PRODUCTIVE –LONG TERM- IF YOU DON'T COME FIRST.** Maybe your TV shows are visiting the gym or going to one movie each week. Whatever. 4-5 hours per week are yours. Start there. Then give to your family. If people live with you, there is a reason why. Be with them face to face an hour per day. They need you (but not as much as you might think or want.) Prior to my truly productive years starting in

1996, I took a lot of phone calls. The most productive people I can think of have all their calls screened, even from relatives. If you take calls, you need to use this time as your Survivor/Apprentice time.

6) I get to sleep. I block out 5-7 hours of sleep. Ultimately, nothing is more important than sleep. Sleep might happen in the middle of the day, before dinner, at night. Whenever. The rule is Kevin sleeps when he needs sleep. I still haven't earned a penny or gotten anything accomplished in this Time Plan!

7) I get to play guitar. I play for about two hours each week....or about twenty minutes every evening. (And...NOW I GO TO WORK.)

8) I do things I don't like to but it's not fun. What I don't like to do is pay taxes, sign contracts, and pay the bills. Bills are paid instantly. Taxes are done when they need to be done. Administrative work is not done by me, if at all possible. If it has to be for you, it has to be. The fact, is that Kevin Hogan needs to be doing things that can't be done by someone else. Focus on challenging, unique Kevin-skill areas. (NOW TO MONEY...)

9) After you get home from the hamster wheel (a job), which rarely leads to anything, it's time to go to work. Work is exciting because it is about you, your dream, your life, your family, your legacy.

10) ULTRADIAN RHYTHM. Break every 90 minutes. Clear the head. Nap 5-20 minutes. Go back to work. This keeps me mentally sharp.

11) KEY TO THE WORLD: LISTEN TO THIS SENTENCE: **I get stuff DONE.**

Most people don't get ANYTHING done. You've heard that: "I didn't get anything done..."

Here's the thing: I get everything done. The focus is on **finish, move it into the pipeline and move on.**

If it is about you, your family, your life, your dreams, your future, get it DONE. Don't put the damn thing on the shelf. To hell with that. DO IT, get it done. That is THE difference between me and the world.

You can be 10 x more productive by simply COMPLETING and FINISHING your projects. THE FAST EAT THE SLOW. Get things done quickly.

10 B+'s are far better than one A. 100 B+'s are better than 5 A's. It's your obligation to serve others well. Do so quickly. 99% of people who write a book will not get it published.

If one person in a 100 who write a book this year get into print, that means I'm as productive as 100 people. Even though they ALL wrote the book. That is totally WORTHLESS. GET THE JOB DONE. Get it in print and SOLD.

They ALL wrote their book. I simply continued the process to the most important thing, which is getting it in people's hands. Life and business come down to influence. Persuasion. Getting someone else to help you make your dream come true in return for something valuable. If you are going to be stressed out, at least get something out of being stressed out! FINISH your work. 90% of work is in the doing. 10% is in the finishing. 100% of the reward is in the completion! **All of the productivity and reward is in the finishing.**

Now, continuing with some suggestions that I do myself, but I write them for you...

12) FINISH (accomplish) as much for your Self as you do the boss you work for. Don't treat anyone better than your family and yourself. Treat all with brilliance and care.

13) Work as many hours for your Self as you do for your boss. The vast majority of people want a job. They are terrified a Chinese woman of 111 years of age will rob them of their job. DUMB. That means you want to build someone else's life dream and ignore you and your kids. How about you pay attention to what matters in life?

14) Continue to LEARN and educate yourself so your value doesn't shrink to the skills of a five year old.

15) You will be productive when you do YOUR life's work. Something that matters. That rewards you. That excites you. NOT ALWAYS THE SAME.

16) Block out projects as far as approximate time. So, a book takes 200 days to write if I write 400 words per day. It takes 10 weeks to get it self-published or 6-18 months to get it published, IF you started selling the book BEFORE

you wrote chapter 2-x. NEVER start something you aren't going to finish. How stupid is that?!?!? And people do it every day. In fact, this is the end result of most projects.

17) If a project is going to profitable, useful, valuable, wonderful, then FINISH it and SELL it. Otherwise you spend 100 or 1000 or 2000 hours doing, being busy and get ZERO productivity. Nothing.

18) The Fast Eat the Slow. Productivity and speed of production are important. How fast can you go from idea to street??? A few days? A few years?

Can you really be 10 X more productive than the average person? Of course. Yes, all it requires is the concept of stubborn completion.

Here's the completion rule:

If you don't finish... you don't sleep or eat!!

Leverage your mind, time or money or both. But notice I did a LOT of projects for which I could pay the Chinese woman $1 per hour to do. I work in labor for therapeutic and health reasons. This I learned the hard way.....I cut my own lawn, do my own landscaping, shovel my own driveway BECAUSE it takes the place of the gym. I don't have to drive to the driveway to get it shoveled and I don't have to catch a bus to the yard to get the grass cut. Sometimes I look at my life and say I'm an idiot. Sometimes I look and think I'm a genius. I always look and know I'm productive.

It really isn't saying as much about you or me as you might think. The average person produces very little. They might be very busy. They might be exhausted at the end of the day. They might have stress coming out of their ears. But they produce very, very little. And it's sad because productivity brings financial reward and financial reward brings the freedom to have time with those you love and the freedom to do what you love.

You've already seen how important confidence is to predicting procrastination. I encourage you to begin to work on your confidence level.

The #1 cause reason for the lack of productivity is refusal to finish. So will YOU put "it" on the shelf? NO. Get it done. Get help to get it done. Get it done TONIGHT BEFORE YOU GO TO BED.

KEYPOINT: Confidence comes with competence and observing your own completion of tasks and projects.

Get a business card with your picture on it. Attach it to a 3x5 card. Tape this card to your computer screen. Write on it, Kevin (or preferably your name!), did you finish the projects you started before doing anything else?

New projects are not to be started until old projects are finished or as far along as possible. Exception: 1-year projects like writing an 80,000-word book must be done *in addition* to small projects.

Now it's up to you. You have the template, and, in this case, an actual script! Most of what you discovered here is counter intuitive or counter to what you were taught in Time Management 101. Time Management 101 didn't work. Don't worry. It wasn't you. It was the system. It was proven NOT to work.

Now you have the solution….live, love and leave a legacy!

The Time Plan System

The system is a series of charts you will use to transform step by step into the mindset of a productive person. The system is extremely simple. And, although you can purchase these sheets for the system online at the web site www.Time Plansystem.com, you can also photocopy these pages for your personal Time Plan.

Step One is Finding Yourself in Time. This step will take you through a complete understanding of what and who are important to you in life. You will make some decisions and priorities. You will find out who the "well-intentioned dragons" are in your life that may need to be jettisoned. You'll become clear about your worries (financial and otherwise) and have a clear picture of the things that are draining your resources. You'll look back over the past decade and discover and clarify your values and beliefs. You'll put an "objective" list of personal qualities together. And, you'll get a clear list of fears and worries. You'll even get clear on your emotional state. By the time you finish the process, you'll have a clear list of changes you'd like to make in life AND the rewards you can expect to receive once you've made your accomplishments.

Step Two is a bit more in-depth. We call it Shaping and Reshaping. In this part, you will delve deeper into your root beliefs. You may want to use a Personal Journal as an accompaniment to this Step. You will find out your personal limiting beliefs and how to blast them into oblivion. You will get a personal boost of confidence looking at your past accomplishments and thinking about those people in your life who are proud of you. Fears and problems will be dealt with. If there are past forgiveness issues, you will face them here. You will get in touch with past dreams and decide what you wish to take into the future with you. You will define for yourself what "meaningful" work is. And, you will have a chance to discover more of your talents and passions! If you have anything that needs repair in life, this is the place to accomplish that – spiritual, physical, emotional, financial. You will figure out what you're willing to sacrifice, and discover what you're preparing to receive as rewards for all you've done! You will conquer any fears of success that may be blocking you. You will choose strategies for success and figure out creative ways to blast through obstacles.

Part Three is called Taking the Task in Hand. In this part, you will utilize the provided pages to begin to chart your actual projects. They will be broken down into Daily Projects, 3-10 Day Projects, and 30-365 Day Projects. You will learn a simple and effective way to prioritize and notate your projects. You will have a place to note and plan upcoming significant profitable projects, as well.

Part Four of the Time Plan System is Optimization and Motivation. Here is where you will decide upon your Time Plan Personal system, whether it be a Daily or Weekly type planner, or even an automated online system. You will receive tips on becoming more organized and maintaining your system. Finally, you will find out how time-productive people stay motivated!

It's important to remain in the mindset, the frame of mind that you have been in throughout this book, or else this will simply be a different kind of planner system that won't work.

For example, you might revise your January **Outcomes and Overcoming Obstacles** (using the charts provided, see below) once or twice each week and not just have this available to you in completed form on December 31. Things change in life. Life is fluid, constantly moving. The goals and outcomes that you have short, medium and long-term, are changing, too.

This is a *good* thing! So, make several copies of charts for each month and keep them available.

The O & O O (Outcomes and Overcoming Obstacles) Charts are not designed to be in-depth tools. They are simply a way to **sketch what you want to accomplish and what is going to get in the way of that.** You aren't writing these outcomes in any particular order. You're simply entering basic information.

So, if this were my chart for January, I would have an Outcome of preparing Power Point for an event I do each year, *Influence: Boot Camp* in March. Obstacles Probable that I might write down are: procrastination and it's possible I could lose all the slides to the computer blue screen and have to start from scratch. Therefore to overcome, I will simply make this a priority for the first week of January to get it done *and* save a spare copy to an external hard drive and USB stick. Simple enough.

The project is simply noted and not prioritized. What is important is noting obstacles and overcoming both anticipated and disaster scenario stuff.

For my work, I have information logged in for each month of the year at the beginning of the year. These aren't goals, these are published plans like events I will give and courses I will train. There are telementoring sessions that are scheduled 9 months in advance, along with books that will be written.

And trips. Business and Pleasure. And things I want to do with my kids.

Get it all down now and LEAVE BLANK space as a reminder that STUFF HAPPENS in life and it WILL HAPPEN. All of that said, I don't want you to think you should have your "year planned out" a year in advance. THAT is crazy. AND it's not desirable.

I don't, and I don't want you to, either!

These are simply outcomes that WILL be WORKED on (or had fun with, it's all the same!) each month. I'm not trying to think of what goes in October the preceding December. This is not a date book. This is what I will be working on in these months. Make sense?

My outcome is not necessarily to finish the Boot Camp Power Point in January, though I will have a COMPLETE set available and a note in February to make updates and upgrades if new ideas occur. I use about two sheets each time I fill them out for a month, and I do this once each week on Saturday or Sunday night.

Remember writing the book in February does not mean the book will be in print in February. Right? It means I'm having fun writing the book in February and that probably fits into my autumn plan of having a release and promotion in September so there will be stuff related to the book in each month. I might get ahead of schedule or (gasp!) behind schedule, which means the Outcomes sheets get updated.

The obstacles are SO IMPORTANT to log because **overcoming the expected and unexpected in life is usually the difference between success and failure.** Seeing the hurricane coming and TAKING ACTION NOW is the kind of stimulus response you want to be able to get out of your brain in due time.

The information in the OOO will get transferred in part to your "daily planner," but for now, this is simply the stuff that you're going to do. I put "Football on Sundays" in September because that's a lifestyle choice that's just as important to me as working on my book. It's not more or less important. It's just going to happen when I don't have an event I'm presenting at...

Once more, **this is not a daily planner, or any kind of a planner,** the OOO is simply a working list which you'll **update**

189

weekly of the things you want to work on, things you want to do, things you have to do. Sometimes you will be working on a project today to finish it or simply to complete some part of it.

Literally, make stuff happen and overcome obstacles. It's that simple.

Confidential

The Time Plan System

Part One

Finding Your Self... in Time

The Time Plan System is really simple to use. You'll **begin here!**

The Time Plan Worksheets

Use these work sheets for the first time you put down your thoughts, feelings, ideas, and dreams. Later you will organize them in a more coherent elegant fashion. You don't need an infallible blueprint to live the rest of your life, but having a general rough draft...an outline...a direction...wouldn't THAT be cool!?

Overview:

There are all kinds of things you want in life and there are all kinds of things you *don't* want in life. AND there are things you don't want, but you have anyway (like taxes, or getting sick). You'll have a time and a place for all these things in living life your way.

You begin with your COMFORT ZONE. **This is life as it is now. This is what you are currently magnetized to.** I've offered some space for logging information in the coming pages, but you're best to have a much less limited amount of space.

You can use your own journal or you can pick up the system by visiting the web site www.timeplansystem.com.

Step One: THE COMFORT ZONE

1. What is going really well in life right now? Life includes everything…business, personal, sex, marriage, partner, your relationship with your guitar, entertainment and leisure, the neighbors are out of town….everything.

2. What is going fairly well, but a whole lot better than it was? It could be better. Stuff/people/work that isn't broken but it would sure be nice to have x.

3. What is going OK, but not as good as it was even two years ago?

4. What is a real mess right now? What is broken? Who is broken? What is the reason it's all still a mess?

5. What else is not working in life right now? Be comprehensive. Marriage? Relationship with kids? Business? Income? Stock returns? Retirement savings way behind? Angry that you screwed up at xyz last month or last year? What stinks? Disease: yourself, someone you love? Child handicapped? IRS? Lawsuit? Lawsuit 2? Partner? Tell me what's going BAD. Circle or place an asterisk by the people/things that are 80% of the bad and the most stressful or difficult for you to cope with, change or handle.

6. *Who Matters* in Life? The question is as blunt as it appears. This is the list of people who matter most to you. The people that are in your life or you want in your life or both. Place a + next to the people you want to please and invest your time or perhaps more time with. Place a * next to people you need to reduce time with. Place a ** next to people next to people who are taking away from living the life you want. Place # next to people who cause you to do good things, or, make you feel good. Some people will obviously have more than one notation. Some people will even have a # and **!

You've now "been where you are." *For all the good and the bad, the familiarity of now is both a resource and an enemy for your future.* Now let's look at what you've been getting ready for... next. These are **decisions** you've made or are currently making. Most decisions and choices can be changed at any time in life.

Step Two: DECISION

1. What are your most important *priorities* for YOU or your life over the next 1-12 months? This includes painting the deck, sleeping 8 hours per day, writing your next book. *These are not questionable or hopeful goals. These are going straight to a DO List.* Don't worry about getting everything "right." Don't even try and get them in order ....just write. You can include things like travel, vacation, take the kids out more, taxes, make time for xyz. Start a new business on the side even though business is good where I'm at? Take *Kevin Hogan's Professional Speaker Course*? You can do all these things, but put the 20 most important here first.

1.

2.

3.

4.

5.

6.

7.

8.

9.

10.

11.

12.

13.

14.

15.

16.

17.

18.

19.

20.

Have more than 20? Write them down....in your journal!

The Payoff

Now, go back to the 20+ priorities and circle 3-7 that make up the 80% of effort you will put forth to accomplish these priorities. You can do as many projects as you want each year, just make sure you always stay in the habit of finishing them and not leaving them on the wayside. The notion of burning up hundreds of hours for having a 0% chance of success on a project, is not one you want to experience any longer! And who might stop you along the way?

It's never easy to get out of orbit. But setting the priorities, both short and long-term, establish triggers. And keeping the fingers on the triggers is pretty important. Your Get To Do List will in part come from these priorities. But there will be people who want to keep you in orbit. I call these people DRAGONS.

Step Three: DRAGONS

Who are the dragons in your life? Who is slowing you down, getting in your way and/or is doing bad stuff to you?

The Dragon Squad

Who sabotages your work?

Who is trying to hurt your life right now?

Who is trying to slow you down?

Who is causing you difficulty in life?

Who is sucking you dry emotionally, spiritually?

Who is taking the life out of your life?

Who is backstabbing you?

Who did I miss and what is the context?

Now, go back and circle (or asterisk) the people that are sucking 80% of your energy that is being stolen from you.....then write them here. Write three sentences about who they are, why they are in your life, if there is anything apparent you can do about them in your life.

1.

2.

3.

4.

5.

Some of your Dragons are "Well Intentioned Dragons." Others are not so well intentioned. Typically, you will need to deal with your dragons. If you don't, you aren't changing your context and your environment. If you stay near too many dragons, you will get burned.

Step Four: THE DRAIN

What financial worries do you have both in the short-term and in the long-term? This year won't be as good as last? Asset protection? Tax related? Fear of loss of current job? What else? Divorce coming… property going? What are the greatest areas of concern for money, present and future, going down the drain?

1.

2.

3.

4.

5.

6.

7.

"Money fears" almost always stem from past behaviors, actions and beliefs. Most of these things don't seem to have anything to do with money.

Step Five: THE DECADE

The Last Decade Summary
Look at the last 10 years of your life and see what describes you.

Which of the following best describes you over the space of the *last* 10 years. (Not today or into the future.)

Pick 2-7 and circle them.

I tend to start a lot of projects but am terrible at finishing them.

I have a lot of unfinished projects.

I tend to finish pretty much every project I start.

I feel relief when I finish most projects.

I feel guilt if I leave a project sit too long.

I've started a number of businesses/projects in the last 10 years that failed (lost money) or couldn't sustain me. (Made very little money or weren't worth the effort. $ / time)

I've started a few businesses in the last 10 years that definitely are worth the time I've put in them from a financial point of view.

I give a ton of money to charity.

I give very little money to charity.

I give money to charity and try to leverage it for business. (Sponsoring a softball team for example.)

I attend a church/synagogue/mosque regularly.

I strongly believe in God/a god.

I think there might be a god, who knows?

There is no question that there is no god.

If you want something done right call a professional.

If I want something done right I must do it myself.

I often trust other people too much. I'm very trusting.

I rarely trust other people and probably could be more trusting.

I don't trust many people and there is good reason.

I trust most people because most people are good and worthy of trust.

In the past 10 years, I've been selling something I believe in a lot.

In the past 10 years, I've sold the best product/service in my field. No question.

In the past 10 years, I've been selling something I don't want to sell.

In the past 10 years, I've found myself selling things that aren't easy to sell because people don't really need or want them.

I sometimes get frustrated because I sell things that aren't always a perfect fit for my customer.

There are changes I'd like to make in my product/service but I can't.

There are changes I'd like to make in my product/service and I have the power and authority to do just that.

What came to your mind while doing this section?

Step Six: THE SECOND OPINION PAGE

If you were to ask the people who know you best, they would say...
Circle those statements below that closely resemble reality and make written notes by them, sometimes indicating an idea with more precision. Other times simply give an example or write down what would be more accurate.

He (*She...*) needs to quit working so hard.

He really busts his butt.

He works all hours.

He never takes time for his family.

He's a great dad.

He really cares about his family.

I wish he had more time to spend with me.

He has a pretty good life.

He has a great life.

He's lucky.

I wish I could live like he could live.

I wish I had what he has.

What else would they say about you, because they probably know you better than you know...you.

Step Seven: THE FEAR LIST

Fear can be the most helpful of all emotions. It can and often does save your life. It also can be the most sabotaging as fear can incapacitate your life like no other feeling. Knowing what you fear and whether those fears are likely to come to fruition is some of the most helpful information you can give your Self.

Fear
The things I fear most in life and business... now are:

1.

2.

3.

4.

5.

6.

7.

8.

Worry is not as incapacitating as fear but it can certainly impact your life in a way similar to fear. Put all of those worries down here and see which of them are most significant.

Step Eight: THE WORRY PAGE
The things I worry most about in life and
business....now....are:

1.

2.

3.

4.

5.

6.

7.

8.

In the course of a day or a week, you and I feel different things and experience different emotions. Arguably, you'd rather experience joy than apathy and prefer contentment to grief. So figure out where you are most often on this thermometer of your feelings.

Step Nine: THE HOW DO YOU FEEL CHART
Emotions and Feelings Chart

How often do you experience the following emotions?
(Always, Most of the time, Often, Sometimes, Not often, Rarely, Never)

Joy

Enthusiasm

Contentment

Boredom

Anger

Hostility

Grief

Shame

Embarrassment

Apathy

Without looking back at any of the other charts, lists or pages, go ahead and write out what changes you'd like to make in life. Be really on target with this list, then compare it to the priorities list and see how you feel about the additions and deletions you noted.

Step Ten: THE CHANGE LIST

You want to make changes in your life. What are they?

1.

2.

3.

4.

5.

6.

7.

You and I need reasons to do the things we do. But we also need rewards. Rewards are extremely important in the Time Plan System because most of the time, rewards are logged into Daily and Weekly Planning before everything else!

Step Eleven: THE REWARDS PAGE
Write down all the things you like to do, get or feel that you want to continue to do in the future. Watch TV? Take a walk daily? Vacations to...where?

Kevin Hogan

Confidential

The Time Plan System

Part Two

Shaping and Reshaping

S eeing how the people, events and experiences of the past have brought you to where you are today is more than a little instructive.

In this section, you gain further insights into where you have been and how that journey has created YOU. Now as you look at the past and the present you can begin to see how choosing the people, places and things you are going to be in the presence of is the single biggest factor in living the life you want.

Each of these experiences or exercises brings to full awareness the impact of how life is like a series of dominos. It's nice to be the one setting the dominos up.

Feel free to print the following worksheets and use them to define your goals, discover your passions, and keep track of your progress.

Step One: From Then to Now – How You Came to Be the You of Today

For this first experience, use 10-20 *Pages in your Journal* until you can mo longer find additional "roots".

Record early life experiences that seem to impact who you have become. Record both first experiences and typical experiences with love (or the lack of), communication (or the lack thereof), and self worth (or the lack thereof). Focus particularly on events that seem to re-stimulate emotions and powerful feelings. Note experiences with beliefs about money, God, obligations, responsibilities, duties, how you parent your children because of how you were raised, how you expect others to work because of how you had to work. Note how you care about people today because of how people cared about you. (You will probably need a dozen Journal pages for this project.)

List the limiting beliefs you likely hold as a result of these experiences:

List the opposite "point of view" or "frame" of these limiting beliefs so they become empowering beliefs:

Step Two: Getting to Know Yourself

Use this worksheet during your quiet time alone, and answer the questions to the best of your ability. Add any of your own insights that may arise during your introspection. There are no right or wrong answers; let your heart lead you.

Who am I?
Why am I here?
What am I meant to be doing with my life?
Looking back at my life, I wish I had:
Looking back at my life, I wish I hadn't:

How could I have done things better in the past?

What can I change about my actions in the future?

Your insights:

Your insights:

Step Three: Your Life

Everyone wants to show someone what they have done, what they have accomplished. In this section you'll find out more about your future as you look at the staggering influence people living and dead have on your life.

Life is.... (write down 10 metaphors or phrases that come to mind) e.g. a bitch, a bowl of cherries, hard, tough, great, etc....Insights into the Edge of the Non-conscious Mind

Talk about five accomplishments in your life that you are personally proud of.

Who else should be proud of you for accomplishing these things?

What skills and abilities do you have that you are personally proud of?

Who do you wish would somehow find out that you really do have these skills and abilities?

Step Four: Your Biography - Overcoming Fears and Challenges

When people read the biographies of people who have achieved greatness there is one common thread that keeps us glued to the story. What did the person overcome?

Look at your life, past and present and see what you have and will overcome.

When someone writes your biography someday, what are the major times, events that they will write about?

What five problems do you have right now that need to be solved before you get to any goal setting?

What are you going to do to solve each of the problems you listed above?

What are five things you fear in life right now?

What are you going to do to solve each of the problems you noted above? What is your plan to face your fears head on?

Step Five: What Life Do I Really Want?

Answer these questions from the heart and quickly. Don't ponder and try to come up with the "right" answers, simply jot down whatever comes into your head when you read the questions.

If I could change my financial situation, I would be doing/earning:
If I could change my health situation, I would:
If I could change anything about my relationships, I would:
If I could change how I see myself, I would:
If I didn't have to worry about money, I would:

If I couldn't fail, I would:
If I could add anything to my life right now, it would be:
If I could remove anything from my life right now, it would be:
More than anything, I want to:
I'm really satisfied with:

Step Six: Forgiveness

So much of our success and failure is dependent upon the people we live with or have spent time with in our life. Over time, strong feelings develop about these people. Similarly there are people, even on the Internet, who have positively or negatively impacted your life. I won't tell you that you must forgive all those people who have caused you harm. I will suggest you consider the possibility. And then, there is forgiving your Self...

I forgive myself for: (ex: things I feel guilty about, letting fear hold me back, not believing in myself, allowing others to define me, allowing others to diminish me, etc.)

I forgive others for: (ex: hurting me, neglecting me, abusing me, belittling me, not believing in me, doubting my abilities, making fun of my dreams, etc.)

Step Seven: Getting in Touch With Your Dreams

When I was a child, I wanted to be:

Do those old dreams still resonate with me?

Today, My Dreams Are:

It's possible that all of your dreams will come true. The fact is that probably won't happen! However, so much of your life is under your control that you can determine how the rest of your life script would ideally play out.

I want you to bridge from dreaming to meaning...and see how they are similar and dissimilar.

Step Eight: Defining Meaningful Work

If money wasn't an issue, my dream career would be:
To me, meaningful work is:
Whose work do I admire, and why?

What qualities would my ideal career have? (dealing with people or long periods of solitude, fast-paced or quiet, logical or creative, etc.)

It is most important to me that my work _____.
(Makes a difference in the world, helps others, makes me feel passionate, serves a valuable purpose, etc.)

Step Nine: Discovering Your Natural Talents and Passions

Most of us have spent so many years focusing on what we "have" to do that we've lost touch with the things we really enjoy doing. These questions should help you to rediscover your true passions. If you can't come up with any clear answers, see the following page for a list of prompts.

I'm naturally good at:
_____ comes easily to me:
People are always saying I should:
I really enjoy spending time:
Some of my favorite hobbies are:
If I didn't have to work, I'd spend most of my time:

My dream life would include these activities:
I've always wanted to learn more about:
If I had the money, I'd take courses in:
If I couldn't fail, I'd pursue a career in:
I want to leave a legacy. It is:

On route to living the life you want, you often have to take a realistic look at what your talents and passions are and see how they match up in the real world.

Step Ten: Prompts for Talents and Passions

There are so many possibilities for things we could be good at, or have a strong passion for. Look over this list and circle the items you've always enjoyed, have a natural talent for, or wanted to learn more about. This is by no means an exhaustive list; some of the items listed might jog your memory for something similar, and if it's not on the list go ahead and add it in the last column.

Writing	Dance	Interpreting	Add
Painting	Acting	Sign language	
Sketching	Singing	Flying	
Photography	Playing instruments	Driving	
Sculpting	Hair styling	Racing	
Shopping	Manicures/ pedicures	Sports	
DIY	Motivating others	Editing	
Computer work	Inspiring others	Proofreading	
Sales	Encouraging others	Broadcasting	
Graphic design	Serving other	Childcare	
Organizing	Fitness	Elderly care	
Communication	Health & wellness	Commentary	
Mediation	Relaxation	Opinion	
Science	Yoga	Designing	

Math	Meditation	Decorating	
Nurturing	Holistic healing	People person	
Gardening	Teaching	Law/legal	
Fishing	Mentoring	Fashion	
Natural living	Guidance	Merchandising	
Website design	Counseling	Programming	
Coaching	Bartending	Human rights	
Coordinating	Host/Hostess	Philanthropy	
Planning	Disc jockey	Weather	
Performing	Catering	Hiking	
Debating	Cooking	Canoeing	
Learning	Gourmet cooking	Research	
Sharing	Baking	Financial	
Simplifying	Cake decorating	Investing	
Sewing	Administrative work	Stocks	
Advice	Administration	Humor	
Dreaming	Managing	Positive thinking	
Planning	Supervising	Speaking	
Taking action	Marketing	Traveling	

Animal care	Leading	Medicine	
Animal training	Religion	Spirituality	
Animal behavior	Philosophy	Crafts	
Language	Metaphysics	Translating	

Step Eleven: Life Repair

From the lists below, identify situations that are out of balance and in need of attention. Circle the items you want to come to terms with, to "heal" or "release," and underline the items you want to strengthen and improve, then list some possible action steps for bringing the situation back into harmony.

Work	Incomplete tasks and projects, overloaded schedule, cluttered office, unproductive habits, unresolved resentment, unhealthy work relationships, unclear objectives, lack of long-term planning, passion, fulfillment, better compensation, more opportunities for advancement, clear purpose.
Plan	

Relationships	Unspoken truths, bitterness, unaddressed anger, grudges, guilt, regrets, dishonesty, destructive behavior, abuse, trust, passion, cooperation, partnership, hope, clear vision.
Plan	
Financial	Increasing income, reducing unnecessary expenses, proper money management, long-term planning, saving and investing, budgeting, reducing debt, collecting monies owed to you.
Plan	

Physical, Emotional, Spiritual	Poor health habits, excessive work, procrastination, work/life balance, recreational time with loved ones, proper rest and nutrition, anti-social tendencies, moodiness, anger, spiritual disconnection, inner emptiness, excessive obligations, lack of purpose or direction, personal time, personal growth, self-improvement.
Plan	

Step Twelve: Qualities I Admire About Myself, and Things I Would Change

Qualities I am pleased to have: (ex: confidence, determination, self-discipline, focus, self-worth, self-esteem, self-assurance, creativity, flexibility, resiliency, vision, patience, courage, self-sufficiency, etc.)

Qualities that need to be strengthened:

Qualities and traits about myself that I would like to be done with and why: (ex: fear, impatience, procrastination, doubt, disbelief, self-disgust, confusion, scattered focus, defeatism, lack mentality, etc.)

Step Thirteen: Sacrifices and Gains

I am willing to sacrifice to gain:

I am not willing to sacrifice to gain:

Step Fourteen: Conquering the Fear of Success

My definition of success and achievement:

Where I see myself going:

Given an opportunity to step into this reality, I might hesitate because of numerous reasons including how difficult it will be to manage current tasks and add in those things required to create a new life. What are all the reasons you might not go where you want to go and be who you want to be and what will you do when you feel those various triggers go off inside of you?

Step Fifteen: Goal-Setting

You've been thinking about them for a long time. Now it's time to put them to paper. Log your goals for all aspects of your life: career, financial, relationships, personal growth, spiritual, physical, etc. Then chunk them down into smaller, more manageable "pieces" for which you will be able to measure your success or failure at each step.

My goal is:	
Measurable Mile Markers:	
My goal is:	
Measurable Mile Markers:	

My goal is:	
Measurable Mile Markers:	
My goal is:	
Measurable Mile Markers:	
My goal is:	
Measurable Mile Markers:	

My goal is:	
Measurable Mile Markers:	
My goal is:	
Measurable Mile Markers:	
My goal is:	

Measurable Mile Markers:	
My goal is:	
Measurable Mile Markers:	
My goal is:	
Measurable Mile Markers:	

Step Sixteen: Choosing Strategy to Achieve

In respect to each goal you "chunked down" into smaller "projects," you now will write out a strategy to manage those steps and to achieve that goal. Use your Journal or these worksheets to identify steps that will cause results, attract opportunities or attention, and noticeable progress.

Step Seventeen: Staying On Target

Write the highlights of your desired life in detail; make adjustments regularly.

List the benefits of your desired life (what you stand to gain):

(Ex: happiness, freedom, abundance, pride in accomplishments, personal mastery and growth, passion, fulfillment, etc.)

Step Eighteen: Creative Ways to Deal with Obstacles

Use your Journal or the worksheet on the next page to come up with creative ideas for observing, experiencing and dealing with obstacles. The next time you feel stuck, review these options and create a plan to move forward again.

Obstacles are:

1) Often predictable and can be prepared for.

2) Often unpredictable and an excellent self test.

3) Something to go under, over, around...

4) An opportunity for a meeting with meaning.

5) Expected on every project you do.

6)

7)

8)

9)

10)

11)

12)

Step Nineteen: Biography: Your Life Chapter Q!

You wrote your biographical sketch earlier. Here write down one story of how you have or will overcome a major obstacle in life.

If it has not happened yet, write your own success story as if it were already true:

List reasons why it is possible for you to achieve what you set out to do:

(Ex: others have done it, you have had smaller and larger achievements.

People rarely tell other people how fantastic, competent and special they are. Look inside and honor your Self.

Step Twenty: 12-Month Outcomes & Obstacles

What follows is not a monthly planner. It is simply a sketch of things you would like to see happen in the coming months; and then, of course, the obstacles that come with the life you want to live!

January _____

Outcomes	Obstacles (Probable and Possible)
What I will do to cause this to happen…	
What I will do to cause this to happen...	

February _____

Outcomes	Obstacles (Probable and Possible)
What I will do to cause this to happen...	
What I will do to cause this to happen...	

March_____

Outcomes	**Obstacles (Probable and Possible)**
What I will do to cause this to happen...	
What I will do to cause this to happen...	
What I will do to cause this to happen...	

April _____

Outcomes	Obstacles (Probable and Possible)
What I will do to cause this to happen...	
What I will do to cause this to happen...	
What I will do to cause this to happen...	

May _____

Outcomes	**Obstacles (Probable and Possible)**
What I will do to cause this to happen...	
What I will do to cause this to happen...	
What I will do to cause this to happen...	

June _____

Outcomes	Obstacles (Probable and Possible)
What I will do to cause this to happen...	
What I will do to cause this to happen...	
What I will do to cause this to happen...	

July _____

Outcomes	Obstacles (Probable and Possible)
What I will do to cause this to happen...	
What I will do to cause this to happen...	
What I will do to cause this to happen...	

August_____

Outcomes　　　　　　　**Obstacles (Probable and Possible)**

What I will do to cause this to happen...	
What I will do to cause this to happen...	
What I will do to cause this to happen...	

September _____

Outcomes	Obstacles (Probable and Possible)
What I will do to cause this to happen...	
What I will do to cause this to happen...	
What I will do to cause this to happen...	

October_____

Outcomes	Obstacles (Probable and Possible)
What I will do to cause this to happen...	
What I will do to cause this to happen...	
What I will do to cause this to happen...	

November _____

Outcomes	Obstacles (Probable and Possible)
What I will do to cause this to happen...	
What I will do to cause this to happen...	
What I will do to cause this to happen...	

December _____

Outcomes	Obstacles (Probable and Possible)
What I will do to cause this to happen...	
What I will do to cause this to happen...	
What I will do to cause this to happen...	

Confidential

The Time Plan System

Part Three

Taking the Task In Hand

T hat was quite a trip. You probably didn't think you had that
much depth and breadth as a person!
You've seen your past, you've made a snapshot of your present
and have laid out a future.

Now it's time to make dreams and desires tangible and real.
It's time to get out of the theater and onto the field of life.

For simplicity's sake I will have you think of today or
tomorrow and write down all the things you get to do, want to do
and have to do.

You've already got a great start at writing your list. Go ahead,
take some time and go back and review all the things you've
prioritized as the most important things and people in your life.
What are they? Who are they? What are things you'd like to "get
to do" with them?

This list will be a very important piece of your Time Plan
System. You will be able to add to it and edit it as often as
necessary. It's best for you to design your own Get to Do List in
your Journal or a personal Notebook, but I've given you some
space on the following page, as well.

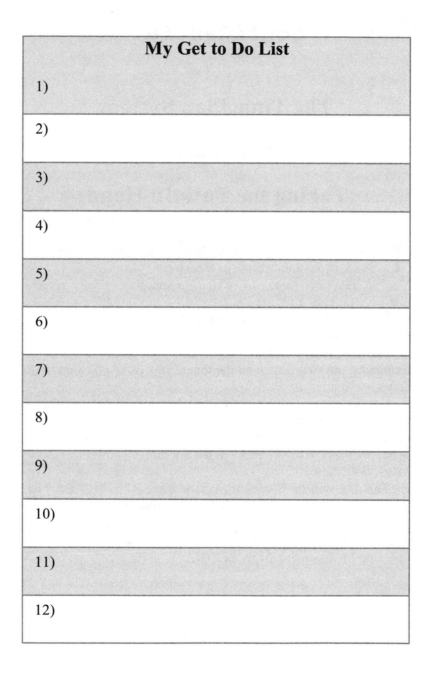

My Get to Do List

1)

2)

3)

4)

5)

6)

7)

8)

9)

10)

11)

12)

My Get to Do List
13)
14)
15)
16)
17)
18)
19)
20)
21)
22)
23)
24)

The next part of your Time Plan System, the Daily Significant Project List (DSPL), is not something that will get stuck hidden in a planner. This is a list you will have on your Coffee Table or desk all day, every day. Each day (or the night before the next day) you'll create a Daily Significant Project List (DSPL).

The Daily Significant Project List

Each day, you have stuff to do.

And so do I. Would you be curious as to what MY DSPL might look like on one specific day?

Well, here's *my very abbreviated* DSPL for today:

** Finish Landscaping Front Yard while Jessica does housework.
*** Finish the Goals Chapter of book.
*** Edit the Procrastination section of book.
**** Coaching call with Rob
** Work on London Gig [Get Thistle to commit to a good price.]
** Write Promo for New York Gig for *Coffee* [New Promo Copy]
**** Teleseminar with Michael for Chicago Gig/Prepare NOTES
** Work on *Coffee with Kevin Hogan*

Now there are a lot of other things that will happen today. I'll play a game with my son, for example. But that doesn't qualify as a PROJECT. That is a DATE. Like a date to go out with your wife or girlfriend. I don't have to prepare for that. I don't have to do anything except BE THERE. A project requires some preparation.

There is a BIG DIFFERENCE in thinking. People get confused between being busy and significance.

Dates go onto your "Get to Do List" and into/onto your daily or weekly planner. However if you have a lot to prepare as far as your date…you might just want to put it on the DSPL!

I have a DATE with my football game on TV on Sunday. I have friends coming for dinner at 5. Those don't require me to think, or plan, or prepare, or research. They require specific time slots on the calendar and planner. AND obviously I can get a lot of work done while I watch the Patriot's play on Sunday 12-3.

Now, notice that on the projects above I have a starred system for each of the "things to do."

That's really important. The key to my system follows…

Prioritizing Projects

**** Top Priority. This gets done. No exceptions. It simply gets done. It's more important than a date with my son. It's more important than that Patriots game. It is more important than eating or sleeping. Only a random act of god can get in the way of **** getting done. Other than that hurricane. No exceptions. Someone stops over to visit? They sit and wait until ****'s are DONE.

*** High Priority. It really SHOULD get done today but it CAN happen tomorrow, but it must be done in the next 48 hours, ideally today.

** Important. This is project work that is very important and has a definite deadline but there is flexibility as to when it can be accomplished. You can let your friend stop by and talk to him if you are working on **. You can't do that with ****. With *** you have to tell your friend, you have a *** you are working on but you want to sit and talk with them for a half hour.

* Coming Soon. This project is something that doesn't need to be done in the next two days but IS coming soon and might as well get it done today if possible. (With the projects listed above, that won't be happening today, but it's on the list, as it will be transferred to tomorrow's list and everyday thereafter until it is completed.)

You'll notice that I list "started" and "completed."

For MOST projects, you will start it today and FINISH it today.

There are exceptions, but my coaching call with Rob is going to happen today. Period. It will not get cut short and spill into tomorrow.

Early on in your use of DSPL you will check off when you begin project x and then check as soon as you have completed x.

CRITICAL: The DSPL SITS ON YOUR DESK or COFFEE TABLE, all day, EVERY DAY, FOREVER.

It does NOT go solely on your computer; it goes on your COFFEE TABLE. When you see the DSPL all day, 24/7, you are always triggered to COMPLETE the project. You can shut the computer off. You can't remove the DSPL EVER.

The two other cards or sheets on your desk are your "Get to Do List" and your 3-10 Day Significant Project List.

Step One: Daily Significant Project List

Priority - Start - Completed
Project Name

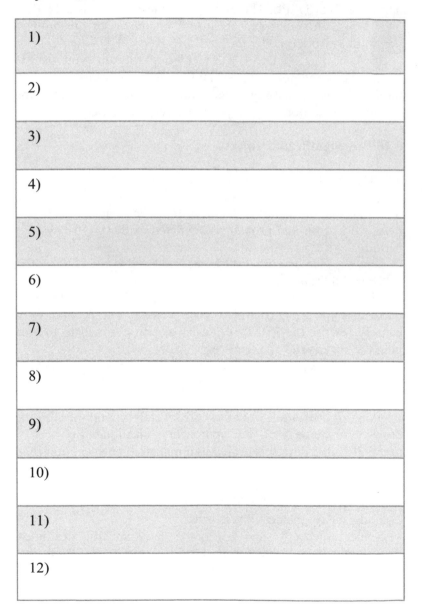

1)

2)

3)

4)

5)

6)

7)

8)

9)

10)

11)

12)

You won't and can't do everything that you want to do today. There are a lot of projects that aren't one day projects but they are still very important. These projects are projects that you might work on today, in fact there is a good chance they will also appear on your DSPL. The tool you will use for this is a THREE TEN DSPL. It's so noted because it encompasses the projects you want to work on over the next 3-10 days.

However, the 310 DSPL lets you log all the stuff you want to do this week and next. The 310DSPL sits on your desk BELOW the DSPL and as new projects come up you record them here. Nothing gets forgotten and everything gets done.

3-10 Day Significant Project List

The 310 DSPL is an extremely important document.

This is similar to the DSPL except that you have looked 3-10 days into the future and noted all of the Significant Projects that must worked on and probably completed in that 3-10 day time period.

There is also one other difference and that is the D2D. D2D is "Days Til Deadline".

This list is matched up against your DSPL EVERYDAY to make sure you are current with your projects. You don't have to entirely rewrite the 310 DSPL daily as you can add to the list until the page is full and then begin again.

You can keep the 3-10 on your computer but you definitely want to keep a paper copy below your DSPL. Guess which I do....

Your prioritization factor is the overall importance of the project combined with the approaching deadline. So **** 5 means that in 5 days this project is completed, no exceptions and it is a top priority.

If you prioritized it as *** 7 it means you don't have to work on this daily but you should put this near the top of your DSPL as in just 7 days the deadline is here.

Some projects ** and * may not have specific deadlines. They might have "best if done by 10"....sort of like milk that needs to be thrown out 7 days after opening it.

Get in the habit of getting ALL projects done AS QUICKLY AS POSSIBLE allowing you more flexibility for DATES. (Time with football or ...even people!)

Step Two: 3-10 Day Significant Project List

Priority D2D   Project Title

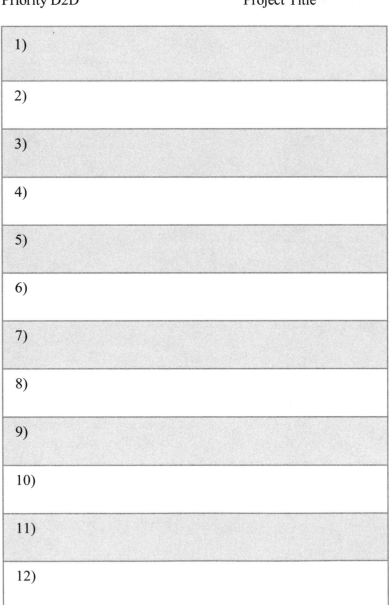

1)

2)

3)

4)

5)

6)

7)

8)

9)

10)

11)

12)

30 - 365 Significant Project List

What projects are happening in the next 30-365 days?

If it's January and you live in Minnesota like I do, then you know the deck will need to be stained come May. There's nothing to prepare for today. You simply note that it's coming up **** May.

Keeping a detailed and prioritized list of all major projects in house, out of house, around the house, for the car, you name it; will make your life easier.

Oil change in ** April. (If it waits 'til May, the car will be fine, but like all projects that are significant, it will need to be accomplished.

My daughter's birthday is not a project. It is a date. (I hope.)

I suggest you make you first 30-365 simply noting all projects that come to mind, onto paper as you think of them. THEN redo the list in chronological order then by priority.

Your notes should look like this:

****July
***July
**July
****August

This is the only list that needs to be redone of the Significant Project Lists. You should create a new list about once each month.

Obviously there's dozens of significant projects in each year so you'll want to have several pages of information. Once it's written down you sleep better because you'll not have to remember anything. It's all there for you.

This list is good to keep on computer, if you like. It is convenient...when the computer doesn't break down, blue screen and end up in the shop.

Step Three: 30-365 Significant Project List

Priority - Month   Project Title

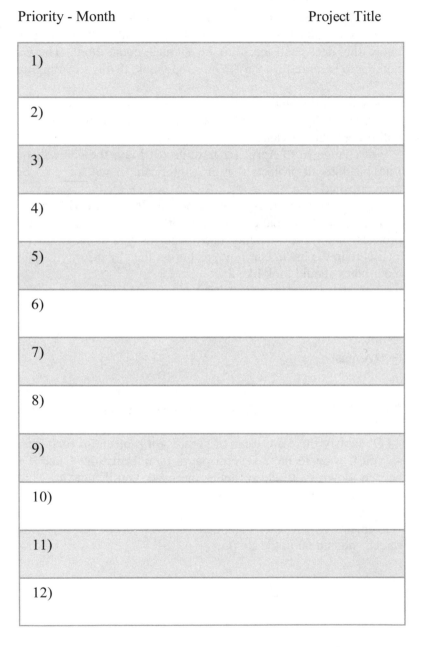

1)	
2)	
3)	
4)	
5)	
6)	
7)	
8)	
9)	
10)	
11)	
12)	

Step Four: Significant Project List for the Future

Priority – Year   Project Title

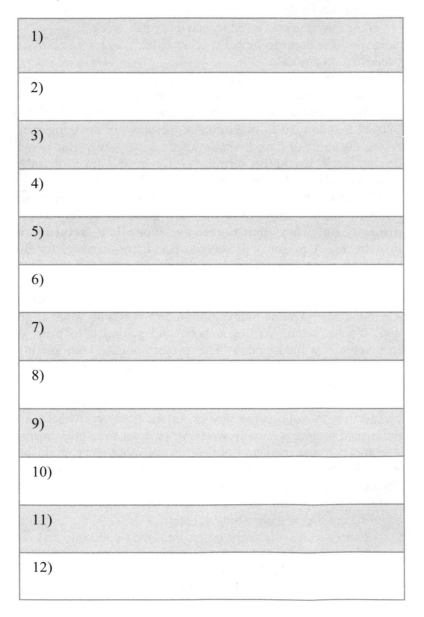

1)	
2)	
3)	
4)	
5)	
6)	
7)	
8)	
9)	
10)	
11)	
12)	

Profitable Project Chart

There are two kinds of projects.

Those that generate revenue, and those that don't.

Some projects don't technically generate revenue for you but are productive in any case.

You have to paint the deck in May. That's two days of work. But it doesn't matter how many days of work it is, it matters how valuable the project is to the future sale of the house. Perhaps $2000? People tend to overestimate the value of anything they do for the value of their home or anything they own. But to not do the deck would be terribly costly at the time of sale. Nevertheless, you don't get credit for NOT being foolish.

One of the big reasons people start projects but don't see them through is they think they are going to be important projects but they don't see an immediate return on investment. A person will stay in their hamster wheel for 30 years if they can't see the value of their projects.

And very few projects pay off this year.

If you write a book, you anticipate being paid in 1-2 years. The book has no value today. And in fact, it has no value at all until it's marketed. Writing a book and getting it in print is relatively ....without value. The project begins with getting people to buy the book. The same is true for many of the projects you'll be working on!

The UPPP Charts will help you keep your projects in perspective to your current work in the hamster wheel. An unfinished project is usually worth $0 or a negative investment. A completed and marketed project on the other hand might be worth $50,000 or $100,000 or $250,000. See how having that number in front of you might move you to act?!

Finally, many projects you do don't have a dollar pay off at any time but they are incredibly valuable.

If I meet with a dignitary or accomplished colleague and do something with them at no fee, I might not be getting paid, but I might be building a bridge that will lead to permanent income.

The same is true in personal relationships, of course.

And, you will need to use judgment in determining which relationships are worth pursuing and which are not.

There two different UPPP charts you can choose from for your upcoming projects. Sometimes you have to remind yourself just WHY you are doing something! That's where the second chart comes in handy!

Step Five: Upcoming Productive and Profitable Projects

Upcoming Productive and Profitable Projects Est. Value in $

Confidential

The Time Plan System

Part Four

Optimization and Motivation

A Get to Do List is your list of things that you get to do! It can be a date with your girl, your kids, friends. It can be going to a show. It can be buying tickets for your vacation. When you first begin using The Time Plan System, you'll keep the Get to Do List distinct from the Daily Significant Project List. The reason is that it can be easy to have one list and check off half the items on the list and then not get projects that bring you closer to the next 10 years of personal freedom completed.

You can have one card or sheet with both your Get to Do List AND Daily Significant Project Lists so you can have one less item on your desk or Coffee Table top. You will see options at www.thetimeplansystem.com

Daily Planner or Weekly Planner

Before we begin: If your current Time Planning System is working optimally for you, keep it. You don't need to change!

To begin, you can automate your planner as part of The Time Plan System. You can check out www.FreeSimpleology.com for that option.

Whether you automate or not, you will always have two things in the brick and mortar world. A journal and a planner do not go into the same binding. These are two separate books.
1) A Journal
2) A Planner

In your Journal you will record your life, your ambitions, your experience, priorities, your frustrations and victories. You will always do this by hand. You can later have this entered digitally but I want you to record life by hand.

Next is a planner. I've created a Planner for you, but first let's look at how you decide what to use.

Weekly vs. Daily

You will either operate off a Weekly Planner and a *Get to Do List* like I do, or you'll operate from a Daily Planner.

The Weekly Planner is perfect for people who live a much more project-oriented life vs. having 5-10-15 appointments and meetings per day. For people who have few appointments, you don't want a planner that will chunk the day down into 15-minute increments. That would be counter-productive. The goal is enhance productivity, not stop it at 4 PM.

If you are an entrepreneur, you will want to work from a Weekly Planner and a *Get to Do List*. If you are in sales or you have a number of appointments, on most days you will work from the Daily Plan and a *Get to Do List*.

Some people will want to use both and that is fine, of course.

If you have a big planning system that you like and you are achieving great things and significantly reducing stress, by all means, keep it.

When I was selling advertising, I used a Daytimer. Sadly, it had limitations. There was no way for me to plan projects for my own business as all that was available at that time was 8-6 scheduling hours, which triggers the non-conscious to direct you toward non-productive activities after dinnertime.

Other systems were physically cumbersome. For someone like me who travels a great deal, I simply didn't have the space in my luggage to have an item the size of a laptop (or bigger) to the mix.

When you pick up The Time Plan System Planner, you'll see how I've adjusted and hopefully responded to the problems and frustrations inherent in the bigger planners.

Your Daily and/or Weekly Planner should not be big and bulky. If it weighs more than a pound, it's probably in need of dieting!

If you are an entrepreneur that is not on a schedule and you require flexibility, then you shouldn't have "time slots" in your planner. Instead the same slot that is for 4 PM today might be 9 AM tomorrow. The flexibility allows for planning projects that you have previously prioritized to make progress on first, then second and so on. A planner that doesn't have preset timeslots also allows for flexible 24/7 planning. I do a lot of interviews at 11 PM or midnight. Sometimes I'm up at 5 AM and working on a project. If I had a planner with preset time slots, it would be two feet tall.

Projects don't get started or finished on a strict schedule. Appointments are required to be started and stopped at certain times. So the style you use will determine the life you are living and want to live!

Finally, I like a Planner that has a Sunday – Saturday layout. Having Saturday and Sunday as the last two days of seven discourages productivity. All of your calendars should be Sunday – Saturday and consistent with your planner.

Optimal Time Planning

Here are some tips you can use to make The Time Plan System and your LIFE, easier, better, more rewarding and more meaningful for you:

- Create a productive work environment.

Have soothing background music or complete silence, whichever you prefer. Have coffee or refreshments available etc. for yourself. Create the kind of environment that allows you to feel relaxed and focused.

- Work at home if you can.

If that means working outside of your house (e.g.: at a library) like I had to do, then by all means do it.

I've had offices over the years but I just hated going to the office. It reminded me too much of school, so, I eventually closed my office door and work from home. No commute time. No lease on an office. No car expenses. (Don't even need a car.) Two hours of time created each DAY is 730 hours per YEAR. Not everyone can work from their home, but you might want to consider it and the extensive tax benefits currently available.

If you are lucky (smart) enough to be a salesperson or entrepreneur, you can take home and earn almost 50% more income by closing the office. (No car, no insurance, no gas, deductible mortgage for 1/3 to 1/2 of the house, inexpensive healthy food and TONS of extra FREE bonus hours each DAY. If you have kids, you'll be there when they get home.)

If that isn't compelling...I don't know what is.

- Optimize a system to deal with "busy" work.

I hate drudgery. Drudgery is anything that I am obligated to do that I really don't like and is almost always a waste of time. Taxes, paperwork, book keeping, yuk. But ya' gotta do it. (Or pay someone to...)

Early in your organizational thinking, you might choose to create your list of what you want to get accomplished during each "work" session. This will help you avoid working in a disorganized manner and create a sense of urgency in you to get everything done. When you approach your work session with a clear plan and sense of purpose, you will automatically feel more focused and energized. You will be surprised with how much you can accomplish just by applying this principle. On the Internet, I know people who have such intense focus that they are able, for example, to put up a website and launch an entire list building and affiliate marketing campaign in only four hours flat. Busy work can be done FAST so you can get to your passions...

Motivation

Motivation is an interesting thing. We are often motivated to learn...learn a lot and then get overwhelmed and quit. It's all pretty simple really: If Jack can do it, you can, too.

The best strategy, is, JUST DO IT.

Without a high level of motivation, it is going to be very difficult for you to get anything done, especially since it takes some time before seeing tangible results. Becoming motivated enough comes down to two things: having a sense of clarity and having some incentive to get you going.

Clarity

Clarity means that you know exactly what you are trying to achieve and how you are planning to achieve it. With all the choices and business strategies available out there, it's easy to be jumping from opportunity to opportunity without really accomplishing anything concrete. You are also going to need to have clear goals. By that I mean tangible goals that are measurable and that you feel connected to (it is realistic enough that you feel you could achieve it). Then proceed to break down goals into sub-goals and mini-steps to help you move forward. Eventually you don't think in terms of goals. You simply write down, "Write new book *Secret Language of Influence."* And then you go do it.

For now, there won't be anything to implement if you do not have clear goals. You need to know what exactly it is that you want. Knowing WHY really helps too.

What kind of lifestyle are you envisioning?

How much would you like to earn?

What type of people would you like to form relationships with?

I could go on and on with different types of questions you need to ask for yourself but I will let you come up with your own.

This process is very important for two main reasons:

- You get a sense of **relief and power** when you know exactly what you are going after rather than shooting aimlessly at whatever life throws at you. You get to control how and where to spend your time, energy and resources.
- You need to be **clear on your objective** if you ever expect to engage in business, whether online or offline. If you don't, you will be drowned under the sea of new information, opportunities and scams constantly thrown at you.

Self-Reward

Another important to do is that you to **reward yourself** for your efforts. (Don't always make it food or you'll just get fat.)

Do not discount this because it is a powerful driving psychological force. It's hard to brain wash yourself if you don't use the classical conditioning methods!

Self-reward, will help your brain create a positive association with the act of getting your work done, and before you realize it you will feel compelled to do it without any self-convincing.

Keep your journal to record your goals and their evolution. It will help you take a step back and analyze your experience more objectively. Your business journal can also be a great source of self-healing, where you can record your fears and doubts, since you most likely will not be able or willing to share this with your relatives or friends.

Efficiency (A.k.a. "Work Hard, Work Smart")

Just about every book in the self-help section now says, "Work smart not hard." That and other idiotic black and white metaphors cause self-sabotage.

Working smart is very important. Working hard is very important. I don't know anyone who has financial freedom who doesn't do both. What you really want is to work efficiently and with complete optimization. You and I get 168 hours this week, so work on the activities that will generate the most return on your time and effort investment.

If you are familiar with the Pareto principle (or 80/20 rule) you know that in most situations 80% of the results come from 20% of the input (or effort).

The trick here is to be able to identify what are these critical input activities that you need to be focusing on to generate most of the desired results. If you make the mistake of allocating most of your time to the other 80% of the activities, which is simply busy work (e.g.: answering most emails) that will only generate 20% of your results, you are setting yourself up for a lot of waste of time and frustration. YUK.

How Not to Get Caught in the Busy Work Trap

You need to identify the most important activities among the maze of tasks you will have to get done for the type of business you are engaged in. You need to allocate your time appropriately to these tasks according to their value in terms of impact on your overall project. When you are able to (or can afford to) consider outsourcing the least critical tasks and focus on the top 20% of the revenue generating activities.

Systemization

One sure way to save time and get your work done quickly and efficiently is to have a set system for as many of your business activities as possible. I think in terms of projects. Whenever you go back on a schedule, you get frustrated because it means you've increased appointments, which have a certain length and no chance for optimization. Having and following the system is advantageous because following an organized set of procedures rather than always improvising makes your life easier, saves time and gives you a sense of control.

Time Management for Real (Stressed) People

There are a couple of ways to consider priorities. There are the priorities that you think about, and, there are the priorities that you don't know about.

How could you not know a priority in your own life?

A lot of people literally focus all of their thoughts on the present. They have their homes foreclosed on, watch their credit ratings tumble and fail to plan to take care of those they love the most. The most important priorities are often those that are not thought of.

How do you figure out what these priorities are today?

1) You ask yourself what's most important in your life?
Your family, your job, your hobbies, your health, your home, etc.

2) Now project yourself out just one year.

How are those things going to be taken care of if any of the others are screwed up? So, if your health goes to heck and you end up in the hospital a chunk of next year, how will you pay for it and how will you take care of your family and future from that point going forward?

If your job situation turns sour? (You were a mortgage banker that didn't make it, for example.)

3) In one year, what actions will you need to be taking to take care of your family, and your future from that point forward?

Nothing wrong with partying today if you have everything paid for, for the next couple of years. If not, it's time to get a plan for the coming year as well as for tomorrow.

People who party today without a navigable plan for tomorrow end up with few good life choices as each year passes. When you don't set priorities in your life, you end up spending a lot of time on things that don't really matter and neglecting the things that do.

Think of it this way....

7-Step Plan for a Realistic Schedule

People who live project based lives are best off *not* using "fixed schedules" in the sense of daily planning time management.

People who work by project may work on two projects today, three tomorrow and one Friday. They might have a random appointment thrown into the mix. A larger family might require at home scheduling for evenings of course.

However, people who live by appointment do need to consider scheduling matters in detail. What follows are strategies, tips and ideas for making scheduling for more fixed schedules both rewarding and painless as possible!

Question: If you could create any kind of daily schedule for your life, what would it look like? You might need to take this exercise to the "weekly level. That's fine. You might also not WANT to have your life on a predictable schedule. That too is not only fine, it's likely for a lot of people. But if you are going to the office each day, you'll probably be on a schedule, at least at the office and because of the logistics of getting there and back it will demand other parts of your life be put on a schedule.

1) Think about how much time each day you'd like to spend working, relaxing, playing, and interacting with others.

2) Now, in order to be THERE in next year, what do you need to do TOMORROW?

If you want a brand new home, you have to have a blueprint, hire the builder, work with the builder and x months later, you can move in. The same is true for almost everything significant in life.

3) Keep going until you've included time for everything that really matters, including time for your family and friends, volunteer activities, creative pursuits, errands and house/yard work, and even television and computer time.

4) Add up the time you'd spend on all these activities daily, and subtract the sum from 24. Do you have any time left over?

Usually one of two things will happen. Either you'll seem to have too much time left over and wonder what you left out. In practice, you'll find that you don't have enough time because you're trying to squeeze in too many activities, or allow too much time for certain activities.

5) Keep tweaking your imaginary schedule until you come up with something workable.

6) Now, compare this schedule to your REAL schedule.

Where are the discrepancies?

What is your real schedule?

7) Each day before you go to bed, note in your journal how you spent each hour of the day, what you did, what you accomplished, how it helped you, your family, your future, your career, etc.

You might be surprised with what you discover.

Family Time

Quality time with your family is important, but it's very easy to shirk when you've got a lot going on in other areas of your life. Instead of promising that you'll spend more time with your family on the weekends when you're not so busy, how about trying smaller segments of quality time more often? A lot of parents live in an illusion that their children are begging to spend all of their time with the parents. They aren't. You want to ask your kids for their input into your decision making process. Have them be honest. That input is one factor that will help you a great deal today and in the future.

Depending on age and circumstance, most kids want to spend some time with their parents each day. Once kids become teens, SOME time as far as duration does matter. But be real. It's not always how much time you spend with your family that creates a solid bond. Quality time is something your family can define.

Personal Time

Unfortunately, this is one thing that usually gets shoved aside when you're busy. You start believing that everyone and everything else is more important than your own self-care, so you keep putting off the things you know would make you a happier and more balanced person. Everyone has to sacrifice x for y in life. In part, that's what LIFE IS ABOUT. BUT don't allow yourself to subjugate all the time.

Time to yourself is absolutely VITAL to your health and well being. It's so important, in fact, that it will often determine your quality of life in ALL other areas! When you ignore your own self-care and focus all of your attention on others and their needs, your energy and focus will suffer greatly.

You might not notice it right away, but you'll eventually find yourself feeling drained, disconnected, scattered and frustrated. If this goes on long enough, the feelings will intensify and begin to affect everything from your job performance to your relationships to your financial circumstances. What other conflicts came up when you were creating your schedule? Make sure you really do know what they are. You will either be in control of your life or randomness and chaos will control you.

Unexpected Delays...Happen All the Time

As much as those who choose to be at an office and work on a schedule might like to believe that they could set a rigid schedule and stick to it like glue, the reality of our lives is much different. Things will go wrong. You will experience unexpected delays that throw off your entire routine. Events will not always comply with our wishes. That's just the way it is.

The airlines, hotels and rental car companies do and will lose your reservations too. Venues will change without you knowing it, your kids will be sick, you will have a 10 hour fight with your partner, etc. Your schedule is a game plan. Just like in football. It has to require flexibility.

One good way to minimize time conflicts is by being sure to allow adequate time for anything you plan to do. You might hope that a trip to the grocery store will only take an hour, but is that what normally happens? You might insist that your commute should take no more than 40 minutes, but what if you encounter road construction or traffic jam?

Get into the habit of planning ahead for the unexpected and allowing a little extra time for everything. If you think something will take 30 minutes, allow 45 minutes, or even an hour. If you do this with all of your activities, you'll find yourself very often being ahead of schedule.

Making Moment to Moment Decisions

Even when you plan ahead, you will likely still have to make moment-to-moment decisions to keep your priorities in order. At the beginning of your day, you might have a clear view of the things you want to accomplish that day. You may have allowed extra time and prepared for the unexpected, but unless you consciously CHOOSE to stick to your schedule in every moment, you will get stuck and get sidetracked.

Example: Your day is going along great. You're ahead of schedule and you just got home from work and are getting ready to prepare dinner. You glance at the clock and see that you've still got another 15 minutes before you would normally begin preparing dinner, and suddenly you feel tempted to get online and check your email - even though you originally set aside an hour for computer time after dinner. Right there, at that moment, you will have to make a decision. Can you trust yourself to stay on the computer for just a few minutes? Or will you lose track of time and throw your schedule off?

What you choose to do in that moment will determine whether the rest of your day continues in a calm and efficient manner, or becomes chaotic and scattered. You can probably imagine endless moments like this throughout the course of every day where you will be tempted to veer off schedule. Whether you choose to do it or not is up to you.

By the way, there is nothing really wrong with not sticking to your intended schedule..... sometimes. You might have valid reasons for doing so, and you'll have no trouble adjusting everything else to work out fine. As you'll eventually come to realize, sticking to a schedule is really all about taking the time to do the things you know need to be done, while still being flexible enough to handle the things you didn't plan on.

Rule. Get stuff done today. Today's stuff doesn't belong in tomorrow's pile. If you do, overwhelm is just around the proverbial corner.

The more you practice juggling the events and activities of your life, the more efficient you will become at handling them smoothly and effortlessly. Of course, your daily activities also include involvement from other people - and that can create another snag if you don't have firm boundaries in place.

Setting Boundaries

If you haven't made a conscious decision to set boundaries in your life, you probably feel overwhelmed by all of the demands on your time. You might have a difficult time saying no to requests from other people, or you might volunteer to take on projects you'd rather not do simply because you feel obligated to help.

Helping others is a wonderful thing - until it begins to take over your life. Taking full control of your schedule will require you to set firm boundaries in your life. This might involve having the confidence to say no when you need to, or summoning the courage to eliminate activities that are beginning to drain too much of your time and energy. Setting boundaries can be an uncomfortable process if you've never done it before, but it does get easier as you go along. Probably the most common problem that arises is your own anxiety about what others will think of you when you say "no."

You might worry that they'll get angry or stop speaking to you. You might feel guilty because you are adding to their burden as you lighten your own, and this can be difficult when the other person is someone you truly care about. What it comes down to, however, is doing what you know is right for you, even if it creates a bit of unpleasantness at first. Take a few minutes right now to glance back over the lists you made earlier.

- Do you see a lot of responsibilities that really aren't yours?
- Do you constantly take on last minute errands or favors for friends and family?
- Do you spend a lot of time babysitting your neighbor's children without reciprocation?
- Are you the one who always ends up coordinating work activities because no one else volunteers?
- Are you the parent who always ends up taking responsibility for school projects because other parents are "too busy?"

You are sacrificing your life for other people...The overwhelm will catch up with you. Stop it...now. When you've finished, consider each of those items carefully. Which of them would you really like to let go of? Which of them is causing the greatest drain on your time and energy? Now for the big question: Are you willing to let go of them? Ask yourself what consequences might arise from choosing to let go of these obligations. The answers might not be pleasant, but would they be worth the peace of mind you gain in return?

Your answer to this question will vary depending on the situation. Some things you might choose to keep simply because you don't feel ready to face the consequences. That's okay! If you are willing to accept the consequences for hanging onto it for now, go ahead and do so.

BE OK WITH FEELING UNCOMFORTABLE in the moment so you can have a BETTER LIFE FOREVER. Build up your courage and get ready to make some waves.

Sometimes IT Really Is NOT Your Problem

When you first begin to set boundaries in your life, you will very likely experience some resistance from others. Especially if you are the type of person that would do anything for anyone regardless of the turmoil it causes in your own life, those people have come to depend on your help.

When you try to give their own responsibilities back to them, they probably won't be thrilled about it. They'll probably react in one of two ways:

Anger and offense. They might express hurt that you won't help them any longer, or try to play on your sympathies by telling you just how stressed out THEY are, and how you are now adding to that stress. They might express anger at you for "not caring" about them, or acting like you NEVER do anything to help them. They might even stop speaking to you for awhile.

Or, they might surprise you by not caring much one way or the other. This can be the most surprising of all reactions, but is more common than you might think! I remember the first time I said no to a request someone made of me. I was apologetic that I couldn't help them but I stood firm with my decision. The person simply shrugged and said okay, then changed the subject. Hello! Who knew it could be that easy?

Of course, it might not always be that easy. But it can happen. Most important in this process is your own commitment to your decision. If you feel uncertain about saying no, they'll probably keep trying to change your mind. If you stand firm in your conviction, they'll know you're serious.

Before you try setting boundaries, you might find it helpful to first get yourself into the right mind-set by reminding yourself that it is not your job to save anyone else. There's nothing wrong with doing what you can to help others, but when it begins to become burdensome and your own life is suffering because of it, you have to make a choice to let it go.

You may also want to explore the reasons why you feel it necessary to take on the burdens of others. Part of the reason might be because you care about them and want to make their lives easier. Or you might be afraid that they won't like you if you don't help them. Do you think that you have to ingratiate yourself to others in order to be liked and accepted? If so, you will continue to let other people influence your time management process. NO ONE can run your life but YOU. So start taking responsibility TODAY.

Finally, remember that this doesn't have to be an either-or situation all the time. Setting boundaries doesn't mean you can't EVER offer to help someone! Instead of blindly agreeing to everything, try a compromise that works for everyone involved. Offer to help with part of a project, rather than taking on the whole thing yourself. Offer to watch your neighbor's kids for a few hours on Saturday while she watches yours on Sunday. Figure out how many hours per week you want to devote to helping others, and then stick to it.

Don't apologize, and don't feel guilty. You have the right to choose how you spend your time. Despite a few people acting like they are losing their right arm, I think you'll be pleasantly surprised by how understanding and supportive most people can be.

Boundaries Require You to Decline

Once you've cleared your schedule of unnecessary obligations, then you need to practice saying "no" on a regular basis so you don't end up right back where you were! Remember, you're probably in the habit of agreeing to do things for other people. It might take some conscious effort to pause and consider each request carefully.

Turning down a request can be as simple as saying, "I'm sorry but I just can't do it right now. I'd like to help you out, but I'll have to pass this time." You don't have to explain why or promise to do something else in the future. Simply let them know that you can't do it, period.

"No can do, book." "No can do, project." "No can do, Inner Circle." "No can do, 24, Survivor, House M.D."

Some people will accept that answer and move on. Others might argue if they really want you to do it, or if they are used to you always saying yes. They might question you in an aggressive manner, or demand to know what makes you so busy you can't help them. You are not obligated to explain or defend your decision!

KEYPOINT: When you finally really "get it" that YOU are in charge of your time, and you really DON'T have to meet the demands of others, you'll experience such an incredible sense of freedom and empowerment.

It's All About Honoring and Taking care of Your Self

Setting boundaries in your life is all about honoring yourself. Having no boundaries means letting other people infringe on your time and energy. Setting boundaries and being firm about them means treating yourself with the respect you deserve.

Conclusion

You can live the life you want. The question is, "will you?"

In order to get there you have to break orbit and that is, of course, the biggest barrier you face. Once you break orbit, you see the world, the universe, to expand the metaphor, through new eyes. It looks and feels very different. It is unfamiliar. Getting to just the outside of orbit requires a lot of momentum.

I believe the tools you've used in this book will get you there.

Now it is time to begin the rest of your life, the life you choose instead of the life randomly assigned to you!

You finish your story, live the life you want and become who you most want to be.

The accomplishments will follow in short order.

I am honored to have been a part of your 168 Hour Week and living the life you want....

Kevin Hogan

Bibliography

Ariely, Dan. 2009. *Predictably Irrational: The Hidden Forces that Shape Our Decisions*. New York, HarperCollins

Baron, Jonathon. 2003. *Thinking and Deciding*. Edinborough. Cambridge University Press

Buzan, Tony. 2002 *Head First*. New York: Thorsons

Covey, Stephen R. 2004. *Seven Habits of Highly Effective People*. New York: Free Press.

Deci, Edward. 1995. *Why We Do What We Do*. New York: Penguin Group.

Deci, Edward. 2002. *Handbook of Self Determination*. Rochester, NY: University of Rochester Press

Deutschman, Alan. 2007. *Change or Die*. New York: HarperCollins.

Dweck, Carol. 2006. *Mindset: The New Psychology of Success*. New York. Random House.

Elliot, Andrew. 2005. *Handbook of Competence and Motivation*. New York: The Guilford Press.

Ferris, Tim. 2007 *The 4- Hour Work Week*. New York: Crown

Frankl, Victor. 1985. *Man's Search for Meaning*. New York: Washington Square Press

Gilbert, Daniel. 2006. *Stumbling on Happiness*. New York. Alfred Knopf

Gollwitzer, Peter. 1996. *The Psychology of Action: Linking Cognition and Motivation to Behavior*. New York: Guilford Press.

Hogan, Kevin. 1995. *The Psychology of Persuasion*. Gretna, LA. Pelican Publishing.

Hogan, Kevin 2006. *The Science of Influence*. New York. John Wiley and Sons.

Kahr, Brett. 2007. *Sex and the Psyche*. New York: Penguin Group

Lakhani, David. 2006. *The Power of an Hour*. Hoboken, NJ: John Wiley and Sons.

Loewenstein, George. *Time and Decision: Economic and Psychological Perspectives on Interpersonal Choice*. New York: Russell Sage Foundation

Masterson, Michacl. 2008. *Ready, Fire, Aim*. New York. John Wiley and Sons

Osborn, Alex. 1979. *Applied Imagination: Principals and Procedures of Creating Thinking*. New York: Charles Scribner's Sons